ENTREPRENEURSHIP

A Tool for Economic Growth
and
A Key to Business Success

ENTREPRENEURSHIP

A Tool for Economic Growth and A Key to Business Success

S.R. BHOWMIK
M.B.A. (Australia)
&
Prof. M. BHOWMIK
M.A. (Econ.)
Formerly Director
P.G.M.B.A. Prog.
Ranchi

NEW AGE

NEW AGE INTERNATIONAL (P) LIMITED, PUBLISHERS
(formerly Wiley Eastern Limited)
New Delhi • Bangalore • Chennai • Cochin • Guwahati • Hyderabad
Jalandhar • Kolkata • Lucknow • Mumbai • Ranchi
Visit us at **www.newagepublishers.com**

Published by New Age International (P) Ltd., Publishers
First Edition : 2007

ISBN : 81-224-1906-2

Rs. 180.00

C-06-08-902

Printed in India at Ajit Printers, Delhi.
Typeset at Pagitek Graphics, Delhi.

PUBLISHING FOR ONE WORLD

NEW AGE INTERNATIONAL (P) LIMITED, PUBLISHERS
(formerly Wiley Eastern Limited)
4835/24, Ansari Road, Daryaganj, New Delhi - 110002
Visit us at **www.newagepublishers.com**

Preface

The book is based on Prof. Bhowmik's pool of experience of long twenty two years since 1973, when the Development commissioner, Small Scale Industry, Government of India, introduced a training program on ENTREPRENEURSHIP DEVELOPMENT for unemployed engineers and commerce graduates for self-employment for the first time in India, followed by a very pragmatic ENTREPRENEURSHIP DEVELOPMENT PROGRAM FOR TRIBALS OF CHOTANAGPUR (now Jharkhand) conducted by XAVIER INSTITUTE OF SOCIAL SERVICE, Ranchi. Prof. Bhowmik, also had the opportunity of conducting Entrepreneurship Development Program of Ramakrishna Mission Lokashiksha Parishad, Narendrapur and the Entrepreneurship Development Program of Tata Steel Rural Development Society, Jamshedpur during 1983 to 1992. He had also the opportunity of conducting entrepreneurship development program along with a dozen of vocational training programs for unemployed youths of Kolkata and adjoining areas during 1993 to 1995. All these above training programmes on entrepreneurship development conducted during 1973 to 1995 by the author gave him a deep insight, diverse knowledge and rich experience on various aspects of entrepreneurship development, particularly in Bihar, West Bengal and Kolkata.

Moreover, Prof. Bhowmik's active participation in many national and international seminars and conventions on Entrepreneurship Development, held in different parts of the country from time to time, and a study visit to Europe to understand the entrepreneurial process of development in some of the European countries funded by the University of Namur, Belgium, generated ample experience and knowledge on the pattern of entrepreneurship development in those highly advanced countries.

The book, deals not only the advantages of entrepreneurship but shows also the pitfalls on its way for creating awareness among entrepreneurs. Vistas of opportunities are there in the country for entrepreneurship development but fanaticism for excellence and consistency of integrity should be considered as the basic qualities for successful entrepreneurs of the future.

Prof. Bhowmik is proud of having a close and personal touch with McLelland, a legend in the field of Achievement Motivation and Malcolm Harper of Cranfield School of Management, UK, an international authority on entrepreneurship development and research.

It is already a proven fact that entrepreneurs of new generation will emerge as a prime force in the economic scene of the country and will be contributing a sizable wealth for the growth of the nation in near future.

S.R. Bhowmik
Co-author

Preface

Acknowledgement

We are immensely indebted to many esteemed authors who have written books on economics, business ethics, human relations, management and managerial economics, marketing and marketing research, financial accounting and book-keeping for consulting their books for our knowledge and information. Since it is not possible to convey our gratitude individually to each of them, we humbly express our gratefulness to all of them from the core of our hearts.

We are also indebted to several esteemed institutions like, Xavier Institute of Social Service, Ranchi, Jharkhand, Don Bose Self-employment Research Institute, Howrah, Tata Steel Rural Development Society, Jamshedpur, Jharkhand, Ramkrishna Mission Loka Siksha Parishad, Narendrapur, Kolkata, Kolkata Youth Self-Employment Centre, Kolkata for drawing wide experience on Entrepreneurship Development because of our long and close association with them.

Lastly we are profusely indebted to many managers of different District Industries Centres of the Govt. of West Bengal for drawing deeper knowledge on Entrepreneurship Development in the grass-root during close contacts with them for a considerable period of time.

Prof. M. Bhowmik

Contents

1

Confidence Building

1.1 WHERE THERE IS A WILL THERE IS A WAY

During a summer hot day, a crow felt very thirsty. He was looking around for water to quench his thirst. He was just wondering. Suddenly he saw a pot in a nearby place from the tree he was sitting. He flew near the pot and took an attempt to look into the pot for water. To his dismay, he found water deep down into the pot to reach his beaks.

The crow thought of a plan to bring the water level up. As he planned, he started with persistence collecting pebbles from the nearby field and dropped them into the pot one by one. The water level came up. The crow drank water to his heart's content. He became happy in attaining his goal and flew away.

1.2 STEPS TO REACH THE GOAL

In order to attain success in life, a person needs desire, vision, determination and courage.

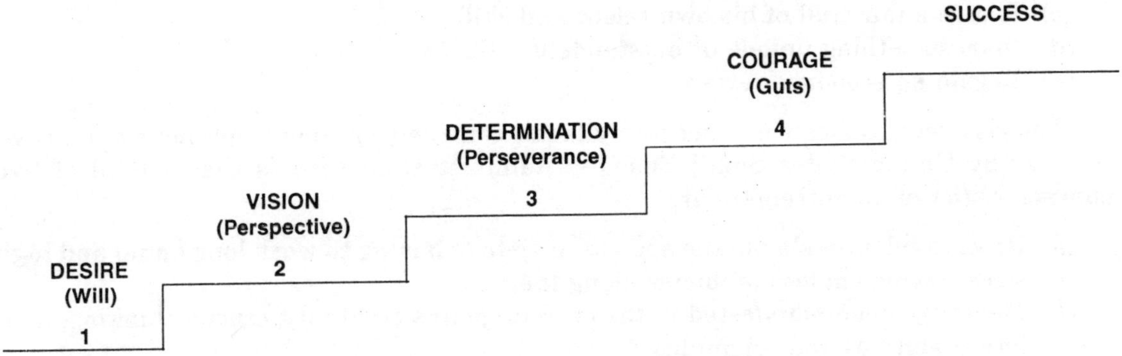

Self-confidence is a powerhouse, which drives a person to achieve his goal. Wealth, talent, etc., are good but it may or may not achieve the dream.

Desire, vision, persistence and guts are the stepping-stones for realization of the goal.

DESIRE: It is something deep in our heart. Something we long for, something we have always longed for and something we will continue to long for. It is the intense desire of a drowning man for a breath of air. But desire without endevour is futile. It must be backed by strong determination.

VISION: It means a great tangible plan: A perspective that foresees the dreamful picture. An achiever must have a vision that he wants to accomplish. The question is: Can we visualize it? Can we hear it? Can we smell it?

DETERMINATION: Persistence is the strongest force that can achieve our goal. One who is tenuously persistent can reach the point. The question is: Do we persist when the going gets tough? When the goal is a little far away, should we quit or get our going with more (intense) diligence? Not only we persist harder but even longer if required to achieve our dream.

COURAGE: It means nerve and guts to go ahead. We should not blink. We look like a daredevil, eyeball to eyeball, to risk. There shall not be an iota of fear of failure within us. What is required is the guts to go forward. Courage is getting away from death by continually coming within an inch of it. The one who dares, wins. We must forge ahead till we achieve.

1.3 ENTREPRENEURSHIP AND ACHIEVEMENT MOTIVATION

1.3.1 Entrepreneurship

Entrepreneurship is the ability to perceive an opportunity, the foresight to see scope for its exploitation, courage to undertake a task, an initiative and dare to take risks in the process of transformation.

There is no difference between entrepreneurship and self-employment. An entrepreneur works for himself, set a goal or target and enjoys satisfaction after achieving the target himself. Major motives that influence entrepreneurs are:

(*a*) To be independent
(*b*) To utilize oneself
(*c*) To give a fair trial of his own talent and skill
(*d*) To do something unique or outstanding
(*e*) To gain an economic reward

The risk reward factor is a necessary factor contributing to entrepreneurial success. A study by United States Small Business Administration reveals that a total of five characteristics of an entrepreneur:

(*a*) Drive to relentlessly pursue success in spite of having to work long hours and high stress facing endless problems along the way.
(*b*) Mental acumen manifested in the entrepreneur's creativity, crucial thinking, analytical abilities and originality.
(*c*) Aptitude for human relations necessary to motivate employees, selling to customers, negotiate with suppliers and convince lenders.
(*d*) Communication skills necessary to enforce effective bi-directional communication whereby ideas and visions are made clear and explicit.

(*e*) Technical ability and strategic management skills to foresee long run and short run implications of critical business decisions, to know one's strength and weaknesses as well as competitors.

In addition to above, a study of the U.S. Small Business Administration has revealed one more vital characteristic: Success of the small enterprise depends on originality of ideas and opportunism. Small entrepreneurs enhance to flexibility and adaptability of economics because individuals move faster than large enterprises. They speed up commercialization process by turning new ideas into new products and services leading to economic dynamism. Enterprise with new ideas and innovation is Entrepreneurship.

1.3.2 Achievement Motivation

In early sixties, McClelland D.C. in his book, "The Achieving Society" has portrayed an n^{ach} person (achievement motivated person) with nine characteristics as follows:

(1) An achievement motivated person likes to take personal responsibility.
(2) An achievement motivated person likes to take moderate risk.
(3) An achievement motivated person wants to know the results of his efforts.
(4) An achievement motivated person tends to persist in the face adversity.
(5) An achievement motivated person tends to be innovative.
(6) An achievement motivated person demonstrates interpersonal competence.
(7) An achievement motivated person is oriented towards the future.
(8) An achievement-motivated person tends to be mobile.
(9) An achievement-motivated person is not completely content.

Mr. McClelland a well known behavioral scientist covered three countries, India, Malawai and Equador under his research project. The major findings of the research are identification of a set of entrepreneurial competencies or characteristics that lead to superior performance. The basic components of entrepreneurial competencies as identified are knowledge, skill, traits and motives.

Knowledge means collection of information. An entrepreneur needs to translate his knowledge into action by dint of his skills because knowledge as well as skills are required to perform a task effectively. A motive drives, directs & select the behavior of an individual. Persons who think about improving their own performance and competing against a standard of excellence are identified by McClelland as n^{ach} (achievement motivated person). A trait includes thought and psychomotor activities related to a general category of events. A person with trait encounters problems in any aspect of life, takes initiative to solve the problem. He doesn't wait for someone else to do it nor expect that luck will take care of it. Therefore, in order to perform any given task including that of launching an industrial venture or any business enterprise and managing it successfully, a person needs a set of knowledge, skills, motives & traits identified as entrepreneurial competencies.

1.4 ROLE OF ENTREPRENEURS IN ECONOMIC GROWTH

Entrepreneural vigour spurs economic growth identifying new fields of economic activity. It is something different from usual practice of business where mostly profit motive is the driving force. On the contrary an entrepreneur has the activity to spot opportunities, secure resources and takes calculated risk to establish a business enterprise.

- Creativity, innovation and diversity of thought are part of the entrepreneur's core value. There are many way's in which a person may be entrepreneur, such as dreaming about new product ideas, new design, new device, new uses to make things more competitive and consumer friendly. This is because he has a natural inquisitiveness, creativity, action, desire and ability to learn.
- In Indian economy, the matter of industrial growth in the initial period had Serious implications for the economy, such as, absence of knowledge about the natural endowments of the country, identification of regional imbalances, low employment generation, inequitable distribution of national income, absence of any concrete policy for mobilization of capital and entrepreneurial skills.
- The small and rural industries are at a distinct advantage as far as the mobilization of capital and entrepreneurial skills are concerned. Innumerable number of small entrepreneurs are spread over semiurban and villages of the country. Large industries cannot utilize them as effective as the small industries. Also large industries cannot mobilize the savings done by people in far distant places. In addition local resources spreadover the country could not be put to an effective use by large industries. In the eighties, it came to light that given necessary credit, power, technical knowledge, a large number of latent resources of the country could be mobilized for the purposes of industrial development and national economic growth. It has been proved that small enterprises are mostly setup to satisfy local needs and these can be dispersed easily. They can also effect a qualitative change in the economy be combating unemployment and gainful utilization of entrepreneurial talent as a tool for growth. This is how the emergence of entrepreneurial genious took place in the country. Initially the entrepreneurship development programmes were taken up to tackle the educated unemployed and engineers all over the country. Special emphasis was laid to tribal entrepreneurship development inclusive of backward communities. The Govt. of India along with state Govts. sponsored entrepreneurship development programmes in almost in all districts. A bold programme on training finance and marketing was introduced to develop entrepreneurship and it was partially proved that entrepreneurs are not born, they can be created by effective nurture.
- It cannot be denied that a number of constraints, such as, deficient managerial and technical skill, inadequate availability of credit, required infrastructural facilities including power, imperfect knowledge of market conditions, are damaging the entrepreneurial spirit. It also can not be denied that there are lack of effective co-ordination among the various support organisations set up for their promotion and development; yet, the nation expects that entrepreneurial success is bound to happen and trigger an amazing economic growth in near future.

1.4.1 Entrepreneurship & entrepreneurs are destined to contribute significant contributions to the country's development process, such as,

- Entrepreneurship stimulates a redistribution of wealth, income and political power within the country.

- Entrepreneurship helps improving the social welfare by harnessing dormant and neglected talent.
- Entrepreneurship results in higher productivity through technical and other forms of innovation.
- Entrepreneurship facilitates the transfer of technology to rural areas
- Entrepreneurship is a powerful tool of job creation by virtue of its labors intensiveness
- Entrepreneurship is a powerful tool for restructuring and transformation of economy
- Entrepreneur creates competitiveness and lead to consumer oriented market.
- Entrepreneur is expected to capture global market by dint of their innovative ventures.
- Long terms involvement with the goal and calculated risk, entrepreneurs create the needs to persist with the enterprise even in the face of adversity. A tendency to analyse the environment on an ongoing basis holds the entrepreneurs in positive and optimistic state.
- As risk bearers, entrepreneurs either succeed and make a developmental contribution or they fail and disappear.

1.5 WOMEN ENTREPRENEURSHIP DEVELOPMENT IN INDIA

A source of inspirations and confidence building

Small enterprises in India having high expectations with limited resources, especially enterprises run by women think of their survival every moment. Irrespective of meager volumes of production, the dedication and involvement along with hard working temper, the women entrepreneurs of India are unique by their class. They are surviving and will survive to acquire a star position in the global market in near future.

India is a proud host of many such small ventures that may be operating on a peanut scale but aspire to turn into big money-spinners in the future. And they are realizing those aspirations by taking effective steps to ensure that they can keep up with vibrant, competitive markets.

The Lijjat story is one such revolutionary case, which proves that conviction and organized labour can produce brilliant results. Lijjat was started in 1959 by seven female members, with a borrowed sum of Rs. 80 at Girgaum in Mumbai who rolled out four packets of papads on the first day.

Self-reliance was their policy and no monetary help was to be sought (not even voluntary offered donation). The seven member pilot team had the ball rolling and now the organisation has grown phenomenally with its Central Office at Mumbai and 62 Branches and 40 divisions spread all over India with a member strength of 40,000 "sister".

It was only the hard work and devotion of each and every sister member involved with Lijjat that made it possible to reach this altitude of success.

Lijjat has adopted the concept of business from the very beginning. All its dealings are carried out on a sound and pragmatic footing, production of quality goods and at reasonable prices. Lijjat presently boasts of exporting through Merchant Exporters to countries like UK, USA, Middle east countries, Thailand, Singapore, Hong Kong, Holland, Australia and other Countries. Jyoti explains, it is unity and strong will power of achieving something great that helps one to be success.

Another good example would be of SEWA (Self Employed Women's Associations), founded by Ela Bhatt, who was working in the Textile Labour Union as a lawyer. Her work experience gave her a finer insight into the daily lives of financially backward women, the forces that over power them, the conditions that perpetuate their poverty, the battle they fight, the attitudes they face and the working and living conditions of both rural and urban working women. Ela Bhatt recognized this immense potential and placed it wisely into the practice of business. SEWA was born in 1972 among the urban poor, with the support of TLA, as a trade union. The process was a fight to forge an identity for self-employed women, as workers.

Although this was a local experience in Ahmedabad, the trouble of home based workers, street vendors; rag pickers were no different than the poor women working in the country all over. Their constant fight to claim their space on the streets, in slums, in the markets and on the planning blue prints of municipal authorities. Vendors as entrepreneurs, home based piece rate workers as producers as they grow ever so organically, they are a true and direct expression of a lively economy.

The emphasis on placing poor women at the center of economic reform, through their unions and cooperatives, is self-evident. There is ample proof in the country to demonstrate that poor women can build strong, vital organisations around issues that are relevant to them, find viable solutions out of their own experiences, and in the process change the society and environment in a healthy, respectful, non-violent and sustainable way.

Centre for Entrepreneurship Development for Women have been functioning in the Bank since 1988. The Centre is serving several objectives for bringing about entrepreneurship development among women. The activities include identify and training women entrepreneurs, conducting Entrepreneurship Development Programmes (EDP) for various target groups, assisting potential women entrepreneurs to start and run enterprise professionally guiding existing entrepreneurs to improve the working and modernization of units, coordinating with the voluntary organisations engaged in promoting entrepreneurship amongst women, helping in marketing the products, assisting formation and credit linking of SHGs and conducting seminars and workshop for the benefit of women entrepreneurs. The Centre has also taking up carrier guidance programs for girl students on business opportunities, awareness on facilities and assistance to women entrepreneurs and providing tips and know how on market survey, preparation of project report and management techniques.

Apart from its presence at the Head Office, 12 search centres are functional at various Circles of the Bank. The Bank, towards providing exclusive banking service to women, has 3 Mahila Banking branches and 6 Mahila Banking Divisions operational at select centers. During the year 2004-05, besides providing counseling to 76,303 women, the Bank had conducted 599 awareness programmes and 682 skill development programmes, benefiting 36,679 and 43,241 women respectively. As at March 2005 aggregate outstanding advances to women stood at Rs. 3,434 crore, forming 5.97% of net bank credit vis-à-vis 5% norm stipulated by RBI. A total of 6,77,581 women were benefited during the year.

1.6 TEN COMMANDMENTS FOR ENTREPRENEURAL SUCCESS

The young generation of entrepreneurs must always keep in mind that their future is highly related with strategic relationship with other people able to develop their enterprise to new heights. The entrepreneurs are found always passionate about their ventures willing to take risk, be optimistic, persuasive, creative and have a great deal of energy for survival. Apart from these qualities the young entrepreneurs must culture ten areas for their growth to success.

1. **Honing of Business Skills:** Learning has no end. As entrepreneur may know many things but he must go on learning business skills to make himself more competitive. He must acquire more knowledge in subjects like new trend of marketing, tactful fund flow management, rigid cost management, performance evaluation, legal skills and obligations and people management. Practical money management, people management and operational management skills are the backbone of any business venture for anyone young or old.
2. **Acquiring New Technology and Processes:** Technology, today is providing tools that entrepreneurs never had ten years ago. It is wiser to include them in their business strategy for the shop floor or in office. They must learn the new language of modern technological process in order to make their enterprise more competitive.
3. **Ingraining Shock Proofing Elements:** Entrepreneurs know that there are many uncertainties and critical situations that can destroy their enterprises. It may come in any shape like sudden fall in sales, deadly cash crunch, or strikes by workforce. In view of these, entrepreneurs must be tolerant against risks than ordinary persons. They must be optimistic and believe that they can solve any problems that may come. They must be shock proof persons and wade through the dark days.
4. **Understanding and Inspiring People:** This is not just a communication skill but to take relatively complex issues and make them easy to understand and to inspire people with one's own vision. It is to inspire people to move in a new direction to attain success with all simplicity and quickly.
5. **Building up Strategic Relationships:** New ventures generally do not have all the required resources or market information to do everything themselves. Working with larger organizations can help them with technology and information to widen their own marketing strategy. Entrepreneurs may prosper by banking their efforts on such strategic relationships without experiencing a sharp learning curve, full of mistakes.
6. **Team-Building:** Combined efforts under an able behaviour is the precondition for entrepreneurs to achieve their success. A good leader knows how to select and motivate the best people. Entrepreneurs, must always realise that an entrepreneurial venture is an organisation, not a single person. They need to focus more on leading their teams rather than micro-managing their enterprises. A successful enterprise is the result of a healthy relationship between the entrepreneurs and the workers. New entrepreneurs need to harness the power of their people through effective leadership above all.

7. **Reward Sharing:** The success of entrepreneurs, depend on the efforts of many people. It does not mean sharing rewards only with people who helped him but giving back something within his own venture. There are many ways to do this. These may be sharing equity, distributing profits, providing bonuses and rewards. It is to ensure that those who helped to create the wealth feel that their contribution has been recognised. This makes them willing and active participators in the activities needed to build up an organization for its optimisation.
8. **Evaluation of Opportunities:** Entrepreneurial failures are high among new ventures because business ideas neglect to undertake basic research on whether it can create a viable and profitable venture. Therefore, before embarking on a new venture, use of evaluation models to test the worth of any new one is a must. Mere business ideas and passion about them may lead to disaster.
9. **Global Operations:** Some small entrepreneurial stars are thinking lately to join the global market. In fact some specialised products, which are in global demand may allure entrepreneurs to build potential ventures to bring them to the notice of global corporations that want to exploit the potential. Catering to international markets ensure growth.
10. **Infinite Learning:** Entrepreneurs must be like sponges. They must always be ready to learn and willing to change the directions if there is an alternative. They must recognise that they can learn from the experience of others and never limit themselves to any fruitful exposure.

The above ten skills will substantially improve the probability of success of entrepreneurs if they are practiced rightly shedding their own pride and prejudices.

2 Organization

2.1 FORMS OF BUSINESS

A business enterprise can be one-man show, a partnership, a cooperative society, a joint family firm or a private limited company. It can also be a Group Entrepreneurship for the rural poor: A new concept in the rural economic development.

2.1.1 Proprietary or Personal Business

In a proprietary business, an individual is the sole proprietor. He manages and controls everything of the business unit. He arranges the capital on his own responsibility and risk and such responsibilities are unlimited.

Advantages

(*a*) It can be formed and operated easily.
(*b*) Organization and operation costs are cheaper.
(*c*) It develops initiative, self-reliance and independence.
(*d*) There is flexibility and directness of control.
(*e*) Trade secrets (methods and processes) are maintained.
(*f*) Unlimited liability helps to obtain credit.

Disadvantages

(*a*) Success depends on skillful decision-making.
(*b*) Unlimited liability is a big risk.

2.1.2 Partnership Business

In a partnership business, a number of individuals associate together for running the business. Partners are responsible to an unlimited extent. They contribute capital and labour to the business and are remunerated according to agreement among themselves. A partnership firm may be registered for the legal safety.

Advantages

(*a*) Unlimited liability is a safeguard against risky ventures.

(*b*) It can be formed and dissolved without much legal formality.
(*c*) It is elastic. It may take new partners if required.
(*d*) Capital raising for the business becomes easy.

Disadvantages

(*a*) Unlimited liability makes it unsuitable for risk bearing enterprise.
(*b*) Dispute among partners may collapse the business.
(*c*) It may be liquidated by death, bankruptcy or retirement of a partner.

Note: The Partnership act-1932 dealt with separately under chapter-VI.

2.1.3 Limited or Joint Stock Company

A limited company or joint stock company is a combination of individuals who subscribe the capital by taking shares of the company.

Advantages

(*a*) Limited liability
(*b*) Vast capital available
(*c*) Greater scope of expansion
(*d*) Transferability of shares
(*e*) Tax Relief

Disadvantages

(*a*) Difficulty and cost of formation
(*b*) Reckless speculation encouraged
(*c*) Clash of interests between members and management
(*d*) Bureaucratic approach may creep in administration

2.2 GROUP ENTREPRENEURSHIP FOR RURAL POOR: A SPECIAL NOTE

Group Entrepreneurship, instead of one individual, is turning entrepreneurship into a whole group of rural people, enabling them to undertake any business proposition, e.g., traditional craft with which they are familiar, and to interact effectively with the market mechanism in such a manner that they obtain a fair price for their product. This will motivate the rural people to see their future in their own village rather than migrating to urban areas.

The great advantage of Group Entrepreneurship is that it can be carried out by the poorest of the poor. Group Entrepreneurship can help them to face the market force from a sound bargaining position and through Group Entrepreneurship. The rural poor can find a place in the organized economy and be productively engaged in the villages by local Agro and Forest based industries.

The concept of Group Entrepreneurship in rural areas has emerged out of grass root work in tribal areas of Chotanagpur, undertaken by the distinguished educationist in the field of management education, Fr. M.V.d. Bogaert S.J. during his tenure with Xavier Institute of Social service (X.I.S.S.), Ranchi, Bihar (Jharkhand).

2.3 FAMILY ENTERPRISE

Today family businesses represents the largest segment in Indian industry and make significant contribution to the economic development of the country. The successful performance of family business can be attributed to its natural resources like commitment, dedication, loyalty, spirit of entrepreneurship, finance strength etc.

Family businesses do suffer also from certain weaknesses like nepotism, favoritism, rigidity, conservatism, etc. These weaknesses can be overcome by adopting certain policies and strategies. The founders may eliminate some amount of family participation to strength the leadership. They should adopt policies to avoid recruitment of family members on the basic of relationship only and do that on the basis of competence. The personnel policies of family business should see equally applicable to both relative and non-relative employees. The routine functions should take place smooth in the face of any major conflict.

In the early nineteenth century, the industrial resolution called for speedy industrial development. This allured a large number of family to promote, build and expand all types of industries which the British got of India encouraged. It is in this context, the family business developed in the early days of industrialization of the country.

The industrial enterprises were the result of joint family effort considering the need of capital investment. Therefore family control continued in the form of ownership and management. In the beginning each family adopted the managing agency system started by the British companies. The system was in the line of need of joint family and took the shape of big family business under managing of envy system. Thus the family business continues to occupy a significant place in Indian Industry.

Family business is the most traditional form of business enterprise. Despite the development of various other forms of enterprise, the family form of business enterprise still dominates. Entrepreneurship, dedication, commitment, family reputation, integrity leadership and initiative are some of the very important qualities of family business. As against the family business, the Professional Management System is being advocated. The Professional Management System helps transform the proprietary firm into a modern corporation in which family ownership and control are separated. It is realized that family enterprise because of its, inherent weakness like nepotism, favoritism rigidity and conservative policies is likely to be vulnerable in the long run. But the existing professional managers have got to prove professional excellence to create an image. Also the supply of professional managers in not adequate in developing countries.

Despite weaknesses of family enterprise, it is still a useful system to achieve pace in industrial development. The unique supply of entrepreneurial and managerial resources from the business family has been responsible for the large-scale success of business houses of the country.

3 Implementation

3.1 WHY SMALL ENTERPRISES?

Small enterprises in every country even in highly technologically advanced countries with large industries have a special role in the national economy on five grounds.

1. Generate employment opportunities
2. Helps in equitable distribution of national income
3. Mobilization of capital and entrepreneurial skills
4. Dispersal of industries
5. Contribution of exports

Rapid economic growth require generation of a large economic surplus in the fields of economic activity. The large-scale industries are generally capital intensive while small enterprises are labor intensive. They have a substantially higher employment potential as compared to large sector. Besides, the simple reason for the relativity higher profitability in small enterprises seems to be the lower wage and greater exploitation of labor on the one hand and fiscal concessions on the other. Moreover when rural industrialization programs are called for to tackle the problems of employment and underemployment, the roll of small enterprises can not be denied.

Small enterprises ensure a more equitable distribution of nation income and wealth under spatial economic development program. It helps removing religion imbalances and decentralization of economic power. It should be recommended that the small enterprises enable a large number of people to share the fruits of economic development. In their absence in rural area (regionally back area) the only option before the people these would be to remain under the poverty line.

Small enterprises have a distinct advantage as far as the mobilization of capital and entrepreneurial skill is concerned. It is a fact that small enterprises can grow rapidly if given the necessary credit, power, technical knowledge etc. A large quantity of latent resources of the national economy can be mobilized for industries growth.

It is expected that with the establishment of large number of modern and technically advanced small enterprises, the contribution of this (small enterprises) sector in export earning will grow outstandingly. Some of the areas which may cater to export markets are readymade garments, sport goods, finished leather products, woolen garments knitwear, processed food, chemical and large number of engineering goods and spare parts. This holds good for all underdeveloped and developing countries.

3.1.1 Advantages of Small Enterprise

1. The very nature of small enterprise is dynamic. It helps in quick decision making and adaptability to changes.
2. Because of small size, effective integration of production and market can be easily achieved.
3. Communication vertical and lateral is fast and distinct.
4. Constant watch on quality is plausible to cater to the needs and requirements of customers.
5. Small enterprises engaged in joint venture and strategic alliances both in national and industrial level may reach global market.

Conversely, there are some problems, which are to be guarded constantly to overcome difficulties that may crop up time to time.

1. **Finance & Credit:** The capital base of small enterprises is very weak and profit earned is often not enough for reploughing. To meet the financial needs, availability of institutional credit must be given prime importance. It is also necessary to liberalize the rules & practices of banking.
2. **Marketing Problems:** All over the world, small enterprises face marketing problems. Most of the small enterprises do suffer from competitive disadvantages, vis-à-vis large industries. Because of shortage of capital and financial resources, these enterprises do not have adequate staying power and are often forced to sell their products at un-remunerative prices.

However, the government and big brothers in the industrial field should extend their helping hands to remove the constraints such as technical obsolescence, inadequate and irregular supply of raw materials, lack of marketing channels, imperfect knowledge of market conditions, inadequate availability of credit, constraints like non-availability of power and deficient managerial & technical skills. Quality consciousness must be generated to the desired level to meet the demands of both the domestic and export markets.

3.2 HOW TO SET UP A SMALL ENTERPRISE

3.2.1 Identification of a Marketable Product

(*a*) Need commercial information and a sound market survey.
(*b*) Need close contact with various concerned organizations, institutions, government departments, chambers of commerce, banks, consultancy organizations and experienced business people in the line.
(*c*) Need to know about the availability of technology indigenously, supply of raw materials and availability of skilled work force.

(*d*) Need to know the total investment, both fixed and working capital for the unit.
(*e*) Prepare a viable market strategy for the product to be sold.

A detailed study is made under Market Information in the next chapter, Chapter 4.

3.2.2 Preparation of the Project Report

After identification of the market and product, a project report is to be prepared by a well reputed organization or by a long standing consultancy firm. Government Organization like Small Industries Service Institute (SISI), West Bengal Consultancy Organization (WEBCON), District Industries Office (DIC) may also be roped in. The main objective is to portray the feasibility and viability of the project with a view to get all sorts of assistances for the project.

Note: A Project Report Proforma approved by the Govt. of West Bengal is enclosed under Appendices.

3.2.3 Suitable Site for the Proposed Unit

(*a*) Availability of the Land (own/rental/lease).
(*b*) Availability of Shed/building.
(*c*) Availability of water.
(*d*) Availability of power.

3.2.4 Registration of the Unit

To avoid any future legal complications, the required legal registration must be done.

3.2.5 Registration Certificate

Registration certificate is a must for obtaining all Government Clearances from DIC, SISI, NSIC. This is because technical feasibility and economic viability of the proposed unit must be vetted by the DIC in the due course.

3.2.6 Financial Assistance

Financial assistance is only extended to the DIC vetted projects and as such direct approach is to be made to any Nationalized Public Sector bank or West Bengal Financial Corporation (WBFC), for the required capital needed.

3.2.7 Documentation Required to be Submitted to Financial Institutions

(*a*) Quotations of machinery, tools and furniture and fixtures
(*b*) Rent Bill from the Landlord if the unit is on rental premises
(*c*) Passport size photo
(*d*) All sorts of certificates e.g., Character Certificate, Technical degree/diploma certificate
(*e*) Ration Card photocopy
(*f*) Trade License photocopy

3.2.8 Availability of Finance

Availability of finance (capital investment) from bank or financial institution must be assured.

3.2.9 Construction of the Building of Factory Shed

3.2.10 Sanction of Power and Water Connection

3.2.11 Permission from Local Authorities

Application to corporation/municipality/village panchayat and other local authorities for permission to establish a unit.

3.2.12 Application to DIC or Proper Authority for Raw Materials

3.2.13 Disbursement of Loans from Bank/Financial institutions Before Starting Production

3.2.14 Ordering Plant and Machinery

Order to be placed for plant and machinery after strict scrutiny of technicalities on approval from DIC, SISI, NSIC, WBFC WBSIC. Procurement of machinery may be done on hire purchase basis.

3.2.15 Completion Certificate of Factory-shed

Completion Certificate of factory-shed or allocation of shed in an Industrial Estate, installation of machinery and plant to be submitted to concerned institutions, banks or Government Departments.

3.2.16 Make Firm Arrangements for Working Capital

Make firm arrangements for working capital from a bank or any other financial institution.

3.2.17 Other Arrangements

(*a*) Contacts for purchasing raw materials
(*b*) Contacts for skilled and unskilled labour
(*c*) Contacts with market (wholesellers, agents, dealers, distributors, etc.)

3.2.18 Trial Run

This is a must for confidence building and first hand experience.

3.2.19 Production Control

(*a*) Processing
(*b*) Checking up finished goods after processing
(*c*) Quality Checking
(*d*) Finishing and get up
(*e*) Packaging, storing etc.
(*f*) Delivery System

3.2.20 Registration with Sales Tax and Excise Department If Required.

3.3 LOOK BEFORE YOU LEAP

A study of a sizable number of small enterprises in India has shown that alarming number of units had to shut down due to the following causes:

Wrong product identification, Inadequate selling, creating a mess in the accounting system, Lack of knowledge in management accounting, inadequate knowledge of tax related matters.

1. Product Identification is no fancy. It must be based on market realities. What to produce at a sufficient margin is a very hard zone. If an entrepreneur fails to identify a profitable product he is sure to dig his own grave.
2. Selling is the life-blood of any entrepreneurial venture. An entrepreneur must understand the meaning of B.E.P.(Break Even Point) of his production. If he fails to do so, he may suffer a long period of gestation leading to collapse of the unit.
3. It is very common phenomena with most of the entrepreneurs that they fail to track down the capital flow regularly. The result is, he will find one morning his liquidity dried up and the whole manufacturing process is jammed.
4. Most of the small entrepreneurs have no idea of management accounting. They do not know even the basic Ratio-analysis to control the fund flow. Nor they have the foresight to engage a financial expert even on part time basis.
5. Inadequate knowledge in tax related matters is another area, which sometimes land them into deep trouble.

The above-mentioned causes may be considered as initial causes of failure. Even then there are more serious causes, which may contribute much more to the ultimate failure. These are:

1. *Excessive fixed assets*: Keeping too much money tied up in land, building and equipment may lead to severe shortfall of working capital.
2. *Inventory trouble*: Overstocking or buying slow moving inventory and spares can be costly and many a times become sheer waste or junk.
3. *Credit collection*: It is observed in many cases that small entrepreneurs have no clear-cut credit policy and regular system of collection.
4. *Location*: Selection of site is vital. If the location is in a place from where finished items cannot reach the customs in time, the unit may run into difficulty.
5. *Competitive strength*: Poor service, indifferent attitude by sales personnel, price cutting to secure the market share may bring disaster.

A potential entrepreneur must be aware of these pitfalls to avoid run outs.

3.4 UNDERSTANDING CONSUMER BEHAVIOR—A CASE STUDY

Analysis of consumer behaviour or consumer research is necessary for arriving at sound marketing decisions. Decision problems presented here relate to all the different elements of the marketing mix and cover issues in product policy, market segmentation, pricing, personal selling, distribution and logistics, promotion and advertising, and development of an overall marketing strategy. The cases illustrate the need for adequate information about the potential buyers, competitive offerings, and the why, how, and where of consumer buying for arriving at sound marketing decisions. Clearly, greater these decisions are based on facts, less chances of making serious mistakes or wrong assumptions. However, it must be understood that consumer information constitutes only the raw material and marketing managements can use it only as aid to their decision making. No research information can ever be a substitute for executive judgement, analysis and discretion.

Vora and Company

In December 1963, Mr. P.K. Vora, proprietor of Vora and Company, manufacturers of Blossom quick-cooking oats, located at Lucknow, sought counsel from the Small Industries Service Institute at Lucknow regarding steps that should be taken to increase the sale of his country. The company had been organized is 1959 and had started to sell its product nationally in 1961; but even by December 1963 it had failed to attain a profitable volume of sales.

Mr. Vora's family had been in the grain business for several generations. In 1959, some four years after, the Government of India had stopped the import of package cereals. Mr. Vora and his family decided to enter the business of processing and selling a product similar to the *Quaker* brand of quick-cooking rolled oats, a product of the Quaker Oats Company of the United State. For some years previous to the Government's embargo, this product had been imported into India by the firm of Muller and Phipps, which acted as sole selling agents. The firm had advertised the product in many Indian cities and reportedly had attained at least a moderate volume of sales, particularly in South India, in the states of Kerala and Madras.

In 1956, shortly after the embargo on Quaker Oats, the Ganesh Flour Mills of Delhi started developing and marketing quick-cooking white oats under the trade mark *Champion*. After some three years of experimental marketing in nearby areas, the Ganesh Mill extended its distribution nationally, devoting a moderate amount to advertising in city markets throughout India.

The management of Vora and Company developed the machinery and method of processing its product on a trial and error basis. The first product offered was not deemed satisfactory by the management and was withdrawn from the market. Not until 1961 was the company satisfied with the product's quality and with its processing equipment, which, when perfected, could produce on a one-shift basis 500 cases a month, each case consisting of 36 tins of 550 grams each. White oats of the finest quality were imported from Australia under Government license. Since Indian grown oats of required characteristics were not available.

The perfected product was submitted to test among consumers and was rated by them as equal to or better than the competing product. The management had made an application for permission to use the mark of the Indian Standards Institution and learned that the product and its processing measured up to the required standards. Mr. Vora anticipated an early arrival of the papers, which could permit the company to place the ISI certification mark on its packages and to refer to the mark in company advertising and selling. He looked upon the ISI certification mark as a valuable aid towards building a reputation in trade and among consumers as to the quality and purity of a product. The competitive product, Champion, bore the ISI certification mark on its packages.

When entering the business, Mr. Vora had no definite data regarding he volume of sales that have been obtained by Muller and Phipps for Quaker oats before the embargo, nor did he know the sales figures of Champion oats. He did know that oatmeal porridge was the leading hot breakfast cereal in the United States and some European countries. He had been informed that the cost of the imported product had restricted its sale, in India, to families with upper middle to high income. Moreover its use had gained wider acceptance in South India than in other parts of the country. From his discussion with agents, Mr. Vora listed the demands for quick-cooked oats, in order of quantitative importance, by regions, as follow: (*i*) Kerala, (*ii*) Mysore, (*iii*) Madras, (*iv*) Bombay, (*v*) Calcutta, and (*vi*) the northern region consisting of Delhi, UP, and Rajasthan.

Apart from the high nutritive value of oatmeal porridge, many people liked its taste when eaten with milk and sugar or with butter and syrup. The quick-cooking oats appealed to many housewives because they had to be boiled for only four to five minutes to be ready to serve, whereas the older variety of rolled oats required about thirty minutes of cooking. Moreover, since the housewife had to exercise to care to prevent the porridge from sticking to the pan and scorching, by stirring frequently, or cooking over a low fire, or cooking in a double boiler, the long cooking oats were less appealing than the new quick-cooking oats. Quick-cooking is made possible by precooking in manufacture after the oat grain had been split and rolled.

Packaging and Trade Mark

Vora and company adopted a round heavy tin package similar to that being used for Champion quick-cooking oats, which, in turn, was presumably patterned after the package in which Quaker oats had been imported. The management adopted the trademark Blossom. The level was printed directly on the tin. The tin had a bright green background with the brand name in large red type at the top of the can. Directly below this was an illustration of several sheaves of oats and a smiling girl. Beneath the left half of the illustration in large white type was the phrase *White Oats* with the word *White* over the word *Oats*. The phrase "Quick-cooking" in smaller type was the right of the White Oats lettering.

The competing tin of Champion oats carried the smiling face of a young boy.

The blossom tin contained 550 grams of oats, the quantity contained in what was thought to be the largest selling package of Champion oats, although the Ganesh Mills also marketed a tin containing 750 grams. Quaker oats had been sold in a 500 grams tin.

The case in which the product was delivered to retailers contained 36 tins. The Champion case also contained 36 tins.

Distribution Channels and Terms of Sale

To secure the distribution of its products, Vora and company appointed agents who generally sold non-competing food products, with exclusive regional rights. For, instance, for Punjab, UP, Rajasthan, Jammu and Kashmir, and the Delhi territory, the management appointed Messrs. R.C. Ramanathan of New Delhi as exclusive agents for the sale of the product to retailers. This firm also handled the products of a large and well-known firm of packaged food manufacturers.

Messrs R.C. Ramanathan were granted a commission of 10% of list price. They had three permanent salesmen covering their territory. In turn, they appointed sub distributors in large towns or cities such as Delhi, Agra, Gwalior, and Mussorie to whom they gave 2% 1/2 off list price out of their commission. Retailers were allowed a trade discount of 10% of

Vora and Company's list price. Thus, the company received from its sales list price less 20%.

The company appointed agent for the remaining states on the same terms. The agents and sub-agents did not act as full-fledged wholesale distributors performing the functions of buying, stoking, and distributing Blossom oats in their territories. They acted rather, as merely indenting agents, taking orders in case lots from retailers for shipment by Vora Company from Lucknow. The agents merely guaranteed acceptance of delivery and payment of orders. Vora shipped its product for destination with bank draft attached to invoice, which was released for the delivery of the shipment on payment of the draft.

Mr. Vora reported that in South India, in Madras, Kerala, and Mysore, which were the largest consumers of oats, sales had been very disappointing. The agent appointed for these states was new to the sale of food products. The agency firm had for some time on sales man of its own calling on retailers, and the sub-distributors appointed with selling rights of various areas had produced very little business for Blossom oats. In the light of sluggishness of the sub-agents, the agent had recently reported the employment of salesmen to push the sale of Blossom oats.

Mr. Vora had not made a practice of visiting his selling agents, but communicated with them by mail.

Pricing

The list price for Blossom oats as on December 1963, varied by section of the country. In North India, the list price of Rs. 81 per case of 36 tins. In Bombay and South India, the price of Rs. 85. As stated previously, the product was sold F.O.R. destination; the commission to agents was 10% off list; sub-agents were granted $2\frac{1}{2}$ of list out of the agents 10%; and retailers were granted a trade discount of 10% off list. Thus, Vora and company received from the sale of each case the following:

In North India	Rs. 64.80 (Rs. 81.00 less 20%)
In Bombay and South India	Rs. 68.00 (Rs. 85.00 less 20%)

Mr. Vora stated that report received from the trade gave the list price of Champion oats in North India as Rs. 93.00 per case. Moreover, he was told that the agents for this product received $7\frac{1}{2}\%$ off list commission and the trade got a discount of $7\frac{1}{2}\%$ from the list. Champion reportedly sold its larger size tins at a list price of Rs. 108.00 for a case of 36 tins. These agents bought and carried stocks of Champion oats in there godowns for delivery to retailers.

Sales

Sales for Blossom oats in the two years following the improvements in the processing had been irregular and had averaged far below plant capacity. For the six-month period, June to November end 1963, then sales averaged only 83 cases per month.

Costs

Mr. Vora gave the following facts regarding his costs per case determined from the accounting data of the June-November period referred to above:

Direct costs per case of 36 tins of 550 gms each

	(Rs.)
Material	24.12
Packing tins	21.60
Other packing materials, wooden case, waterproof	
Paper, box strapping pads	4.00
Direct labour*	5.40
Railway freight	4.80
	59.92

Overhead costs

Monthly overhead costs were stated to be as follows:

	(Rs.)
Rent	165.00
Electricity and water	50.00
Coal	50.00
Depreciation on plant @ 6%	
(Rs. One lakh investment)	500.00
Interest on working capital	250.00
	1015.00

* Mr. Vora's monthly wage bill was Rs. 900, but the work force was used for nearly half of the time on another project in which Mr. Vora was engaged. In the light of the irregularity of production, the labour cost given is probably high as compared with what it would be if the plant were operating at or near capacity.

When this overhead was allocated against the 500 case sales of the period, the overhead costs came to Rs. 12.18 per case.

In the above figures, Mr. Vora did not include any salary for himself.

Advertising

From the time when the national distribution of blossom oats was started, the selling agents had urged Mr. Vora to advertise. For some months he under took such advertising in the major cities in which he had sales representation. After spending some Rs. 4,000 without any apparent sales response to justify such expenditure he ceased advertising.

While Mr. Vora had suffered considerable loses since the launching of his enterprise, he was still anxious to make a success of it and was willing to put more money into the venture if the suggested chance for his marketing gave promise of bringing profitable sales.

Source: Indian consumer: Case study by Professor Subhas C. Mehta Indian Institute of management, Ahmedabad.

3.5 FORMULATION OF A PROJECT REPORT

A project report is meant to provide the necessary information which may be required for the purpose of processing the proposal for getting the financial assistance. The report should be prepared in such a way that is able to provide a complete framework for the presentation of all the information that would be required by financial institutions for appraising the project. The following are the broad heads under which the complete information on relevant aspects should be included in the project report meant for a S.S.I. project:

3.5.1 General information.
3.5.2 Project description.
3.5.3 Market potential.
3.5.4 Capital costs and sources of finance.
3.5.5 Assessments of working capital requirements.
3.5.6 Other financial aspects.
3.5.7 Economic and social variables.

3.5.1 General Information

Under this head some information of general nature should be provided such as:

- Name and address of the entrepreneur.
- Qualification, experience and other capabilities of the entrepreneur. If there are partners, characteristics of all the partners individually are to be provided.
- The constitution and the organisational structure of the enterprise. In case of a partnership firm, whether it is registered with the Registrar of firms.
- Whether a registration certificate from the Directorate of Industries has been obtained or will be applied later on.
- The utility of the product and the range of products to be manufactured.

3.5.2 Project Description

A brief description of the project covering the following aspects should be given in the project report:

3.5.2.1 Site	Location whether owned or leasehold land. Whether the site is in approved industrial areas.
3.5.2.2 Physical infrastructure	Availability of physical infrastructure consisting of the following items.
3.5.2.3 Raw materials	Which are the source of raw material and what is the probability of getting it on a continuous basis at fair prices. If imported raw material is required, whether license has been obtained for that.
3.5.2.4 Skilled labour	Whether skilled labour is available in that area!
3.5.2.5 Power	Information regarding power requirements, stability of supply of power and the price at different consumption levels.

3.5.2.6 Fuel	Whether other fuel items like coal, coke, oil or gas are required and if yes, then their availability position are to be stated.
3.5.2.7 Water	If water is an important factor for a project like brewery or soft drinks, the source and quality of water should be clearly stated.
3.5.2.8 Waste disposal	Most industrial plants produce waste materials or emissions of various types like (*a*) Gaseous (Smoke, Fumes etc.) (*b*) Physical (noise, heat, Vibration etc.) and (*c*) Liquid or solid discharged through pump and sewers. The aspects like scope of dumps, sewage system and sewage treatment plant should be indicated.
3.5.2.9 Transport facility	Availability of different transport facilities should be stated.
3.5.2.10 List of Machinery and equipments	A complete list of item of machinery and other equipments indicating their type, size and cost should be stated. Sources of supply of capital equipment and the construction services should also be given.
3.5.2.11 Capacity of the plant	The installed and license capacity should be stated.
3.5.2.12 Technology selected	Whether the technology selected is up-to-date and appropriate? Which other units are using the same technology and with what results?
3.5.2.13 Manufacturing Process	The stage of production and the process involved should be clearly stated. The period of conversation from material into finished goods should also be mentioned.
3.5.2.14 Quality control	Whether some system has been designed to check the quality of products on a continuous basis? If there is a probability of getting quality marks like 'ISI', 'Q' or 'Agmark' for the products, the fact should be included in, the project report.
3.5.2.15 Research and development	Besides quality control, whether any cell to study for the improvement of quality is proposed to be formed in the enterprise should be stated.

3.5.3 Market Potential

The following aspects relating to market potential should normally be covered in the project report:

3.5.3.5 Total demand and supply of the product	Data regarding total expected demand of the product and the level of present production are to

	be stated. How much of this gap can be filled up by the proposed unit.
3.5.3.2 Estimates of cost of price	An estimate of manufacturing and administrative expenses together with the price expected should assess the margin of profit.
3.5.3.3 Marketing strategy	What strategy for selling the products is proposed to be followed? Whether arrangements have been made with reputed suppliers and distributors for lifting the production.
3.5.3.4 After sales service	For some products after sales service is most essential. Arrangement made in this regard should be stated for such products.

3.5.4 Capital Costs and Sources of Finance

An estimate of the various components of capital items required by the unit should be given in the report. These components may be the following:

(*a*) Land and building.
(*b*) Plant and machinery.
(*c*) Other miscellaneous assets.
(*d*) Preliminary expenses.
(*e*) Contingency against price rise.
(*f*) Margin for working capital.

3.5.5 Assessment of Working Capital Requirements

While estimate the capital costs, margin for working capital will have to be taken in to account since the unit will be able to function only when adequate working capital funds are available. To be more precise, at the initial stage itself, the estimate of working capital requirements should be made and shown along with the total cost of project which should include value of all other forms of assets such as:

(*a*) Stock of Raw materials
(*b*) Stock of finished goods
(*c*) Semi-finished goods
(*d*) Money to be received from customers for the goods sold to them on credit.
(*e*) Cash to be maintained for day-to-day expenses.

Business the cost factors, if the report does not include on assurance of present and probable source of finance, it will serve no purpose. Unless the resource availability covers the requirements of funds for the factors stated above, no banker would like to accept a project. The estimation of funds for the cost factors involved should be very realistic and correct, since may units run into serious financial problems just because of inadequate estimates of funds requirements made at the initial stage or at operational stage.

3.5.6 Other Financial Aspects

One of the objectives of settings up a project is to earn a livelihood. This would be possible only if the products taken up for production are profitable after retrieving the investments made within its life cycle. This would required preparation of a project profit and lost account which would indicate likely sales revenue, cost of production, allied costs and profit. It is also a good idea to show the break-even analysis along with the report.

3.5.7 Economic and Social Variable

Under this head the costs for controlling the environmental damage, the number of persons proposed to be employed and need for sub-contracting function of such type that ancillary industrial units may be promoted to meet them, should be covered.

Submission of the project report

Finally, as mentioned earlier, sources for financing the cost of the project must be identified. The fixed capital can be financed to the extent of about 75% to 80% by way of 'long term loan' from SFC or Commercial Banks. The funds for working capital to the extent of about 60% to 75% of the requirement may come from Commercial banks as 'Working capital loan'. If the unit is coming up in a backward area, a capital subsidy to the extent of 10% to 25% of the fixed capital may be sanctioned under the Central subsidy scheme depending upon the location and the Government policy for that location. The entrepreneur's own investment should be around 10% to 20% of the projected cost which may come from either his own deposits or from loans from friends and relatives. The loan component should not exceed 70% to 80% of the total projected cost as far as possible. Depending upon the nature of machineries used, depreciation should be calculated at a rate ranging from 10% to 20% of the value on machinery and the rate of 5% of the value on buildings.

CONCLUSION

A project report incorporating all the above information may be prepared in consultation with institutions like SISI, T.C.O, DIC and SIDC who later on recommend them to the banks. Besides these institutions, several commercial banks also render assistance in this respect.

3.6 CONSIDERING TECHNO-ECONOMIC FEASIBILITY OF A PROJECT

An entrepreneur has to formulate a project. It is a process whereby he makes an objective and independent assessment of various aspects of an investment proposal. The first stage of project formulation is feasibility analysis from both the angles of technical as well as economic considerations. The concept of technical feasibility denotes adequacy of the proposed manufacturing process and plant and machinery to produce a given product largely within the frame work of predetermined quality specifications, raw material and utility consumption level and out put quality per eight hour norms, without long or expensive breakdown problems.

Every feasibility analysis is different and is tailored to identify the strength and weakness of the project.

Techno-economic Feasibility refers to the estimation of project demand potential and choice of optimal technology. It makes an analysis of the market and technology. The choice of technology itself will be based on the demand potential and aid in project design.

Techno-economic Feasibility analysis gives to the project an individuality and sets the stage for detailed design development.

The factors to be considered while preparing a techno-economic feasibility report are:

3.6.1 Technical Consideration

(*a*) Know-how sources of know-how and payment of royalty/patent rights.
(*b*) Process and quality control description of the selected manufacturing process, showing detailed flow charts and presenting the alternative process and justification for the adoption of the selected process.
(*c*) Determination of the plant size, production schedule with expected volume for an eight-hour norm.
(*d*) Selection of machinery and equipment including specification, equipments to the purchase and its origin, quotations from suppliers, delivery schedule, term of payment and spare-parts availability.
(*e*) Plant location and a design of the plant layout.
(*f*) Report on availability of raw materials, terms of payment, process of supply and continuity of supply.
(*g*) Estimate of labour requirements and the supervision guidelines.
(*h*) Indication of type and quality of waste to be disposed of, waste disposal methods and necessary clearance from proper authority.
(*i*) Estimating of production of the product.

3.6.2 Economic Consideration

1. Market region to be covered, of market survey done copy to be enclosed.
   (*a*) Major competitions in the field.
   (*b*) Competitive edge in terms of price, quality, publicity, sales campaign, etc.
2. Selling arrangements: sale, organisation set up appointment of sales representatives, machinery for collection of foils, if sales is arranged through distributors/sole agents and their names and addresses, their experience in the line, organisational setup commission payable, credit period, period of contract, advance payment, if any to be made.
3. Financial Projections:
   (*a*) Projections of performance and profitability
   (*b*) Break Even Analysis
   (*c*) Details relating to the assumptions on which the projection on profitability made
   (*d*) Assessment and Computation of working capital.
4. Investment:
   (*a*) Cost of fixed assets proposed to be acquired and working capital requirements and other expenses.
   (*b*) Detail picture on bank loans, own investment and government margin money.
   (*c*) Credit on purchases.

5. Security: In addition to the industrial assets of the unit, details relating to any other assets offered as security.
6. Labour Position: Recruitment/availability of skilled/unskilled personnel for the unit.
7. Repayments: Proposed schedule of repayment loans with required startup period.
8. Ratio Analysis: Types of ratio analysis to be applied—Liquidity Ratio, Activities Ratio, Profitability Ratio, Leverage Ratio.
9. Managerial competence: It includes
   (*a*) Classification of tasks as per organisational structure
   (*b*) Grouping of activities into tasks
   (*c*) Activity analysis involving anticipated
   (*d*) Determining inter relationship between different positions to decide the Chain of Command
10. Implementation Schedule: It is prepared to ensure timely completion of the project. It helps in saving time and cost. An implementation schedule includes when to apply for term loan, procurement of land, site construction of factory shed, getting water and power connection, purchase of plant, installation of plant, requirement of labour, trial production and time for commencement of commercial production.

4

Basics of Business Operations

4.1 MARKET INFORMATION

An entrepreneur needs to collect a variety of data and information to make his product proposition viable. A general guideline is laid down below.

(*a*) Try to generate as many ideas as possible, which can be usefully commercialized. Ideas may also be generated by observing functioning of similar business units in the field. A close discussion may also be held with them in order to assess particularly the dark-side of their experience.

(*b*) After making a short-list of products that can be technically and commercially exploited, an endeavor should be made to meet concerned officials of SISI and DIC initially to sort out viable ones. Such discussions should be based on entrepreneur's own strength and weaknesses. It may appear that some products are attractive but the same may not be commercially exploited or technically feasible. In the scale of operation planned. In some cases banks and financial institutions may not encourage on ground of absence of the requisite expertise to make it on economic scale.

(*c*) Certain products may require long gestation period before they start yielding profit. In such cases, the idea may have to be dropped.

(*d*) Sometimes financial parameters do dictate selection but such ideas must be rigorously examined by Ratio Analysis with the help of financial management experts.

Generally selection of products is based on

1. Own/partner's experience in the field
2. Product identification based on expansion or diversification plans of ongoing business
3. Products which are likely to have a ready market either in local or regional market
4. Products which show high profitability
5. Products based on certain specific advantages available from reservation of product lines for small scale industr[illegible]

6. Sometimes concessional finance or other resources, incentives are being made available by government
7. Product lines guided by changes in certain field of industrial policy, specially licensing policy
8. Sometimes products are identified from the list of items exported
9. Occasionally government also invites to produce items indigenously as import substitution.
10. Small items and spare parts required by railways may also be taken up for production
11. Small items required by Indian Coal mines have enormous scope for production
12. Recently defense items, particularly for aviation purpose have a very bright future in view of short supply of aviation spare parts from overseas.

However it is fully admitted that identifying a product is a difficult process and sometime wrong identification may lead to grave results. Therefore every case should be taken in the matter taking into consideration all sides of the problems that may crop up subsequently.

4.2 MARKET SURVEY

Market survey means systematic collection, recording and analysis of existing or potential markets, marketing strategies and the interaction between markets, market methods and potential products/services.

Market Survey Objectives

1. What is the size of the market and market share anticipated for a product?
2. What is the pattern of demand?
3. What is the market structure?
4. What are the buying habits and motives of the buyers?
5. What are the strong points of the business unit in marketing ?
6. What are the past and future trends of the market?

How market survey can be utilized

1. Market survey for selection of the product (product identification).
2. Market survey on availability of raw materials, price and delivery of the same.
3. Market survey for machinery and equipments.
4. Market survey on competitor's strength and weakness.
5. Market survey on consumer behavior and motives.
6. Market survey for assessing demand and supply of own products and preparation. of production schedule vis-à-vis the market.

4.2.1 Market Survey Proforma

A simple proforma may be prepared on the basis of the following questions:

Group-A Questions

1. Who are the buyers in the existing market?
2. Who could be the potential customers?

3. What is the area and market share of the product in the existing market?
4. What do the buyers need, require and expect?

Group-B Questions

1. Who are the competitors?
2. What is their area of operation?
3. How are they organized?
4. How much market share do they command?
5. What are their strengths and weaknesses?
6. Do the competitors' product over shines in any way? What are they?

Answers from the above set of questions of Group B will clearly bring out the startling differences of competitors' products, hence corrective steps may be taken accordingly to improve the product.

4.3 PRODUCTION PLANNING AND QUALITY CONTROL

Management is required to map out a well-arranged Program of Production by weaving all the factors into an integrated plan that may result in qualitative, speedy and economical manufacture of products. Workers are made to do the work as planned and arranged for, and all the physical facilities like materials, tools, machines and jigs are arranged by management in advance.

This advance planning result in greater volume of work, lesser cost of production, shorter time of manufacture and more certainly in the execution of orders.

1. **Production Planning:** Production planning is concerned with three considerations, namely, how, when and where the work is to be carried out. But mere planning or without planning does not ensure that the actual production would confirm to planned activities. It is the production control that directs the flow of production in order that products are manufactured in the best and cheapest method, that they confirm to the desired quality and they are ready for sale at the right time. For this reason, management chalks out a definite course of production, fixes up the time schedule within which production is to be completed and pursues the production line till the completion of manufacturing.

   The following are the 4 steps involved in production planning and control:

   (*a*) *Routing*: Routing involves the determination of the way in which products are to be made and the selection of the path over which materials are to be worked out into finished products. The object of routing is to determine the best sequence or order of operations to be followed in the manufacturing process. Routing also designates the proper tools, equipments and the requisite personnel to be used in the process of production. This routing indicates the sequence of operations and the machines and tools required for production.

   (*b*) *Scheduling*: Scheduling is the fixation of time and date when each operation is to be commenced and completed because of the varying lengths of time required for the production of various parts or components, priorities are to be fixed to operations which take more time than others, or operations which are associated with the possible break down of machines and rejection of products.

(*c*) *Dispatching*: Dispatching is a function, which initiates the actual production as planned by previous two steps of routing and scheduling. Dispatching gives the necessary authority to start the routed and scheduled work and for this purpose, it issues orders, instructions and information relating to the work. Dispatching involves the allocation of materials, labour force, and machines for the execution of the production orders.

(*d*) *Inspection*: The maintenance of quality standards is an important work of any production control system. Finished products are subjected to an exacting nature of inspection with a view to confirming the quality of production to a predetermined standard. Defective or faulty production is rejected by the process of this inspection.

2. *Quality Control*: Quality inspection of finished products is insufficient for meeting the demands of standardized mass production. As inspection is concerned with determining the acceptability of products after manufacturing, it can neither ensure the fabrication of high precision products nor prevent the scrapping of finished products on a large scale.

Quality control is not mathematical but statistical. So, statistical quality control is designed to regulate in process manufacturing and to take corrective action in such a way that products confirm the quality standards. Inspection is not replaced by statistical quality control, rather it is put on a broad based quality system by the introduction of statistical devices.

The modern quality control system has three distinct functions viz: acceptance, prevention and assurance. Determining the acceptability of finished parts or products is a function of inspection, while the other two functions are encompassed in statistical quality control. Preventing quality variations from established standards and assuring quality maintenance within defined limits of errors are the two functions, which center round the quality of conformance. The quality of design is, however, beyond the scope of statistical quality control and dealt with inspection.

Statistical Quality Control (SQC) secures cost reduction in a number of ways. It saves labour and material costs involved in scrap and rework losses, leads to greater production by economizing the use of materials and labour, reduces inspection expenses and resulting in securing better prices through the elimination of downgraded products.

The majority of the products confirm to the quality standards because of the correction of assignable cause variation, while some products deviate from the standard for chance causes which are uncontrollable.

3. Work Measurement: The improvement of work should precede the measurement of work. Several methods can be adopted such as: Stop-watch time study, Predetermined systems used, Work sampling etc. Stop-watch time study has received considerable criticism and work sampling method is receiving increased attention. Work sampling is based on sampling theory. It involves the breaking down of total working time of all workers who perform the operation into instants of time that are used as the basic unit for sampling. The exact instants of time for actual observation are determined by some random method. After the observer tallies the action occurring at a large number of different instants of time, the total number of instants at which each type of activity has been observed is divided by the total number of observations. The results are the percentages of instants at which each type of activity was observed. These percentages are the basic data provided by work sampling. They yield directly the information needed for determining allowances.

4.4 PRODUCT COST, BEP ANALYSIS AND PRICING

Product Cost: Costs are the expenses involved in production of goods for sale or providing service. It may be defined by keeping a set of accounts which will classify and allocate expenditures appropriately and will also show the total cost of any particular unit of production without a reasonable accuracy.

Cost accounting shows the cost of each process, each component and finally the cost of the finished article. Costing shows, which type of output will be profitable and which type will not and how the final goal is achieved.

4.4.1 Aims and Objects of Cost Accounting

1. Classification as par nature of expenditure in production.
2. To ascertain the unit cost which will help to determine the selling price.
3. Efficiency can be increased by comparing the actual cost and estimated cost.
4. Helps the management by supplying the necessary information to take decision on their policy and planning.

4.4.2 Elements of Costs

Costs are divided mainly in two classes:

(1) Direct Costs
(2) Indirect Costs

It is applicable to all parts of expenditure incurred in production, administration, sales and distribution.

Direct Costs: are those expenditures that can easily be identified or directly attributable to a particular product in the process of manufacturing.

Indirect Costs: include all other expenses, which are not directly attributable to particular product, under manufacturing. It is known as overhead and considered as indirect cost.

4.4.3 Expenditure

As a whole, expenditures can be classified in three broad heads:

(1) Amount spent on materials
(2) Amount spent on labour
(3) Other expenses.

The above expenses may be incurred direct or indirect way for any particular unit of production.

The divisions of expenses incurred may be as follows:

1. Direct Material + Direct Labour + Direct Other Expenses = Direct Cost or Prime Cost
2. Indirect Materials + Indirect Labour + Indirect Other Expenses=Indirect Costs or Overheads

Indirect Costs or Overheads are spread over on the entire business organization like in production, administration, sales and distribution. But direct costs are incurred in the production sub-system only. The indirect costs incurred in the production sub system are called "Factory Overheads". The entire expenses on administration sub system are indirect expenses.

The formula for Product cost is:

1. Manufacturing Cost = Prime Cost (Direct Cost) + Factory Overhead
2. Product Cost = Manufacturing Cost + Administrative Expenses

4.4.4 Break Even Analysis

Definition: The Break Even Point is that quantum of sales at which the unit is just able to recover all expenses. In other words, it is the point at which neither a profit is made nor any loss incurred, i.e., No profit - No loss, just the pointing level of activity that the unit should operate at.

Example: A unit manufacturing pencils, sell each pencil for Rs. 2.50. Material cost per pencil is Rs. 1.50 and fixed costs of the business unit are Rs 10,000 per year.

Contribution from each pencil = Rs. (2.50 – 1.50)
= Rs. 1.00

The total contribution required to meet the fixed expenses is therefore Rs. 10,000. Thus the unit should sell at least 10,000 pencils per year to break even, more than that quantity sold will be indicated as profit.

4.4.5 Calculation of Break Even Point

Expenses incurred by a unit can be classified into two categories i.e.,

(*a*) Fixed Cost
(*b*) Variable Cost

Fixed cost is that cost, which does not vary or change with other factors in the production level for a considerable period of time.

Variable Costs: Variable Costs are those costs, which vary with the volume of output and are directly related with the production.

Variable Costs = Product Cost – Fixed Cost
Calculation of Break Even Point (BEP)
BEP = {Fixed Cost(FC)/ Sales Revenue – variable Cost} x 100%

$$\text{or BEP} = \frac{FC}{SR - VC} \times 100\%$$

Pricing: Price is the governor of marketing activity, since Sales are mainly circumscribed by the pricing of products. Price is determined by the top authority/executives of units in such a way that it may bring the largest volume of sales with a sufficient profit margin. A number of considerations are involved in the pricing of products.

First, the price must be high enough to cover all the costs of production, but at the same time, low enough to attract customers.

Secondly, the extent of competition that a particular line of product has to face in the market often influences the pricing of products, for the sake of competition, varying margins of profits may be required to be fixed for the different products of an enterprise.

Thirdly, the, marketing process calls for the determination of several prices for different parties, viz, wholesale price, retail price and consumer price. These price differentials must be satisfactory to all parties, otherwise traders may not push the goods in the market and consumers may be driven to products of other concerns.

4.4.6 Unscientific Pricing: A Gambling

Besides the above universally accepted norms, sometimes a manufacturer may fix up a price in three ways:

1. Price fixed above the line (standard market price)
2. Below the line
3. As the market bears

Some producers think that if the price is kept above the line buyers may consider the products offered are genuine and quality products for which they gladly pay more. In this case the producer may get higher price but there is a chance of lower sales. Some other producers think that if the prices are kept below the market, sales will record high as the buyers will be happy to get products at lower price. Unfortunately price-cutting may be a curse in disguise for considering such products as of poor quality. The third category of producers who think to sell products at a price, which the market will bear, may face a tough competition. This may require an aggressive sales campaign, publicity and advertisement.

However these unscientific pricing processes should not be taken recourse to jeopardize the good will of the organization.

4.5 SIMPLE INVENTORY CONTROL

Meaning of Inventory Control or Stock: It is defined as systematic location, storage and recording of goods in such a way that desired information and services can be made available to the operating shop at minimum ultimate cost.

The Need for Inventory Control: As per the definition, inventory control is nothing but systematic maintenance of a reserve of goods, that will ensure manufacturing according to a production plan based on sales requirement and the lowest possible ultimate cost. It is to promote smooth factory operation and to prevent piling up of an idle machine time, proper material must be on hand when it is wanted. Proper inventory control can reduce such losses to a great extent.

Essential Steps in Inventory Control: It is essential that the necessary materials shall be on hand when required and no more store shall be preserved that is necessary. The following four standard procedures are followed to control inventory:

1. The maximum of stores
2. The standard order
3. The minimum of stores
4. The ordering point

4.5.1 Advantages of Inventory Control

(*a*) It creates buffer between input and output.
(*b*) It ensures against delays in deliveries.
(*c*) It allows for a possible increase in output.
(*d*) It ensures against scarcity of materials in the market.
(*e*) It utilizes the benefit of price fluctuations.

Economic Lot Size: It depends on two groups of costs:

(*a*) Preparation costs which are mainly fixed costs
(*b*) Carrying costs, which includes interest on capital, insurance, obsolescence, deterioration, handling, inventory taking etc. Numerous formulas have been developed on this. The oldest and the least known one is:

Q = 2RS/I in which
Q = Economic lot size
R = Annual use of the items in units per year
S = Setup cost each time a new lot is started
I = Carrying cost per unit per year.

ABC Analysis: ABC Analysis segregates all the items of stores into three categories: A,B,C on the basis of their annual usage. "A" items covers hardly 5% to 10% of the total items but account for 70% to 75% of the total money spent on the material. These items require rigid control and to be stored in smaller quantity. It needs procurement frequently. "B" items generally cover 10% to 15% of the total items and represent 10% to 15% of the total expenditure of the stores. "C" items covers 70% to 80% of the total items. They represent hardly 5% to 10% of the total annual expenditure on stores. The categorization is so made to enable the enterprise to pay the right amount of attention in the area of inventory control as merited by the items A or B or C.

4.6 SIMPLE ACCOUNTING PROCEDURES, FINANCIAL FORECASTING AND PLANNING

There is some income and expenditure in our regular life. Most of the people keep records of all income and expenditure to know the actual financial position. It is not compulsory for an individual in family life, but in the case of a businessman it is compulsory, rather statutory obligation.

To a businessman, or a business unit whether small or large, account keeping is necessary for the following reasons :

1. For Self Satisfaction: To know the actual position of a specific period, say an account-ing or financial period. For example: 1st January to 31st December (Calendar Year). 1st April to 31st March (Financial Year).
2. Statutory Obligation: Accounts for the specific period should be submitted to Income Tax, Sales Tax and authorities as may be required.
3. Record Keeping: For entry of day to day transaction, proper administration and financial control.
4. Management Information Service: To know the details of investment in assets, position of liabilities, turnover, profit ratio, budgetary control etc.

The Essential Books of Accounts, that are necessary for a small business unit :

1. Cash Book
2. General Ledger
3. Purchase Register
4. Sales Register
5. Stock Book

Some useful terms in Accountancy :

1. Transaction: Any type of give and take, which can be converted in money value is called transaction because this will change the financial position of belonging parties.
2. Accounts: It is a brief description of transactions with an individual or personal business unit in relation with personal or business property or a nominal business income-expenditure, profit and loss etc.
3. Turnover: It is the total sales value or earning of revenue arising from sale of products or services for a specific period.
4. Debit account: The account, which takes the amount of transaction.
5. Credit account: The account, which gives the amount of transaction.
6. Entry: When transaction is written down in books of A/C that is entry.
7. Ledger book is a book where different A/C heads are maintained.
8. Cash Book or Cash A/C: Where all cash transactions (receipt or payments) is written down and the A/C head in cash A/C.

The following evident are required to maintain books of accounts :

(*a*) Cash Memo: Documents of Cash Purchase/sale

(*b*) Bill: Documents of credit purchase/sale, which raise the claim of purchase/sale value.

(*c*) Challan: Documents for transit of goods from one place to another place bearing proper signature.

(*d*) Money Receipts: Documents of money receipt/payment. This document is issued after receiving money in any type of transaction.

4.6.1 Accounting Procedure

In a type of business, accounting procedure will be as follows:

First step is recording. For each transaction, proper evident or documents will be collected and on that basis first entry will be done in respective books of A/C.

Second step is classification and condensation. It is also a posting staged from first entry and record.

Third stage is summarization. In this stage accounts finished and the position of business will focus through profit and loss A/C and balance sheet.

4.6.2 Book-keeping

In the case of a very small business, where a regular accountant cannot be employed full time, the entrepreneur should maintain an Income and Expenditure account regularly. It is necessary to maintain financial control over the business with full knowledge of debtors and creditors position. It is an informal books of accounts with all entries of daily income and expenditure including debtors/creditors receipts and payments. It should also include all types of personal investment/expenses. This book is only for personal record but not presentable to any Authority. The entrepreneur must engage a part time qualified accountant to make out Presentable books of accounts out of the informal book of accounts as mentioned above. Formats of the formal books of accounts are shown below:

I. CASH BOOK

Dr.					Cr.				
Date	Particulars	L/F	Amount (Bank)	Amount (Cash)	Date	Particulars	L/F	Amount (Bank)	Amount (Cash)

II. TRIAL BALANCE FOR THE YEAR ENDED

Particulars	Dr. Amount	Cr. Amount

III. TRADING ACCOUNT FOR THE YEAR ENDED

Dr.		Cr.	
Particulars	Amount	Particulars	Amount

IV. PROFIT and LOSS ACCOUNT FOR THE YEAR ENDED

Dr.		Cr.	
Particulars	Amount	Particulars	Amount

V. BALANCE SHEET AS AT

Liabilities	Amount	Assets	Amount

4.6.3 Financial Forecasting and Planning

The financial planning function involves long range plans for plant expansion, replacement of machinery and equipments and miscellany of expenditures causing large cash drains.

Financial forecasting and planning demand attention to the following areas:

1. Financial analysis that ascertain the capabilities and needs of the concern.
2. Prediction of the needs for funds over the short run operating period with attention devoted to cash flows, cash budgets and sources of current capital.
3. Prediction of the need for funds over a long run period.

Financial analysis consists of a comparison of a firm's current status with industry standards. It points out the firm's operating weakness, its potential capacity, the volume and type of financing needed to enable the firm to accomplish the objectives of the management.

A checklist for comparing the performance of a firm with the international norms is shown below:

Name of the Ratio	***Formula***	***International Industry Norm***
I. Liquidity Ratio		
Current Ratio	(Current Assets)/(Current Liabilities)	2.6
Acid Test Ratio	(Cash and Equivalent)/(Current Liability)	1.0
II. Activities Ratio		
Inventory Turnover	(Sales)/(Inventory)	7 times
Net Working Capital Turnover	(Sales)/(Net Working Capital)	5 times
Average Collection Period	(Receivables)/(Av. Sales per Day)	20 days
Total Capital Turnover	(Sales)/(Total Assets)	2 times
III. Profitability Ratio		
Gross Operating Margin	(Gross Operating Profit)/(Sales)	30%
Net Operating Margin	(Net Operating Profit)/(Sales)	6.5%
Sales Margin	(Net Profit after Taxes)/(Sales)	3.2%
Return on Capital	(Net Profit after Taxes)/(Net Worth)	7.5%
Net Profit on Working Capital	(Net Operating Profit)/(Net Working Capital)	14.5%
IV. Leverage Ratio		
Debt to Equity	(Total Debt)/(Net Worth)	56%
Current Liability to Net Worth	(Current Liability)/(Net Worth)	32%
Fixed Assets to Net Worth	(Fixed Assets)/(Net Worth)	60%

4.7 CHOICE OF TECHNOLOGY

Decision on what to produce and how to produce are central to all other elements of operations strategy. Product feasibility is carefully assessed before a product is designed. The primary concerns in product design relate to standardization reliability simplification, reproducibility, maintainability and modular design. Process determination consists of evaluating a series of decisions on the alternative ways of producing a product, the type of technology to adopt the plant and machinery to be used, the work flow system for the product and the method of performing the job.

Before taking up the process selection issue, the fundamental question to be considered is whether to make or buy the product. Make or buy analysis provides the planner with the comparison whether to produce or buy. The major aspects that determine process are technological and sequential. Technology means a combination of labour, machines, processes, energy and other inputs directly involved in the transformation of materials into products. Technology has increased the outputs of industrial and also non-industrial sectors. It has improved the quality and reliability of the products and saved the capital costs. Technological considerations occur at two levels:

(*a*) general technological feasibility technology and
(*b*) specific choice of equipments.

General technology feasibility may be thought of decision regarding the theoretical feasibility of making the product, the general nature of the processing system and the specific equipment to be used. Sequential considerations are those that aim at determining the most efficient relationships between processing steps. Firms using existing technology should maintain a continuing interests in improving it as long as changes are economically desirable and can be justified. Increasing the output rate, reducing unit cost, and improving the yield are the motives for seeking improvements in existing technologies. Various criteria for evaluating production process and equipment selection are:

(*a*) Product requirements
(*b*) Technological feasibility
(*c*) Financial considerations
(*d*) Labour and skill requirements
(*e*) Output and capacity needs
(*f*) Compatibility with existing facility
(*g*) Flexibility
(*h*) Raw material requirements
(*i*) Size & weight limit, imposed by plant or building
(*j*) Maintainability
(*k*) Spare parts inventory requirements

The selection of the most desirable technology can be aided by tools like economics analysis, capital investment analysis, linear programming, marginal analysis, breakeven analysis and incremental analysis. Motion and time study, work standards and work measurement are the aids for integrating the human factors in process equation.

4.8 IDENTIFYING BUSINESS OPPORTUNITIES

Investment opportunities are always in the market. How to choose the right one? Some of the basic guide line to explore and evaluate the pros and cons are shown below:

1. Market survey and contact with friendly business personality.

2. Vistas of opportunities according to Govt. Guidelines both Central & States.
3. Contract with big industrial houses for ancillary or feeder industry development.
4. Visits to trade fairs & consultation of trade journals.
5. Product lines emerging out of new technology and scientific progress.
6. Product lines coming up due to change in consumption pattern due to modern life-style and living.

Whatever the opportunity identified, everything to be analysed from the viewpoint of technical feasibility, economic considerations and commercial viability. Before the game starts, an entrepreneur must plug all loopholes against self-ruination for life. What to produce at a sufficient margin is a very critical area covering all aspects of a business. Thereafter, comes selling and sales management. If an entrepreneur take long time to reach his BEPoint means he may suffer a long period of gestation leading to collapse. He also has to be alert about the funds flow with all accountability. Otherwise he will find one morning all his liquidity is dried up and the whole manufacturing process is jammed. He must acquire the knowledge of ratio-analysis to control fund flow. There may be many other causes related to the identification of product line to enter into. Focal points to be examined before selection of the product line are:

1. Collection of basic information evaluating those facts and figures.
2. Market survey
3. Approaching business people already in the failed for checkup.

4.8.1 Commercial Information

Sufficient commercial information relevant to the proposed item of production must be collected, such as:

(*a*) Potential demand in the market
(*b*) Volume of such demand
(*c*) Knowledge about competitions already in the field
(*d*) Assessing future demand
(*e*) Infrastructural facilities – water, power, transports
(*f*) Availability of raw materials
(*g*) Location selection dictated by the nature of the product itself
(*h*) If an ancillary item is selected, the assistances offered by the parent industry to be discussed clearly and with specific assurances
(*i*) Expected return on investment is the prime factor to be assessed
(*j*) Environmental factors.

4.8.2 Market Survey

All the relevant ingredients like raw materials, equipments, selling, distributors, consumer behavior etc., should be taken into account so that no loose end remains.

(*a*) **Equipments** – this needs information relating to manufacturers (indigenous or foreign) of the equipment, competitive feature of manufacture products, price structure, repair, maintenance and after sales service, requirement of technical and skilled labour and their supply, and delivery of the machines and equipments.

(*b*) **Marketing and distributions** – selling directly or indirectly, rather selection of most advantageous channel of distribution is one of the most vital choices of the predacious. It is the blood artery of the business. It must flow unclogged. Advertising and publicity programme to be taken up as per resources permit. Every rupee spent in publicity of any kind including demonstrations should be assessed and analysed as to weather they have any effect or not on sales. Market practices on credit facility, minimum order, incentives, rewards are also to be critically examined to control waste or excessive financial burden on producer/manufacturer.

(*c*) **Consumer behavior** – Understanding consumer behavior and devise sales message are the fundamentals of marketing. Analysing buyer behavior and their purchasing power is a precondition to profitable marketing. Roping buyers by their motives by explaining to them about the quality, price, durability, service should be the basic aim to reach the desired goal of the producers/manufactures. The basic objective of any producer/manufactures should be to ensure consumer satisfaction and always look for newer and more effective ways of reaching a costumer. Entrepreneurs must have a clear vision, goal and objectives well defined. Besides, constant feedback of results are essential for improving the product and performance. Any producer or manufacturer should provide value for money to the customer. This helps to gain the market share eventually in the long run.

So far attempt have been made step by step approach to opportunity sensing. The question comes to the mind of an would be entrepreneur interims of "whether this is a line for me or not or do I have all that the line would demand". An opportunity which does not result into a business or industry is not an opportunity. It is just a vague idea.

A small case may perhaps illustrate this two friends Roy and Das were traveling from Asanol to Calcutta by a day train. On their way after Asanol their train stopped at Burdwan. Young teenagers with packets of roasted peanuts crowded the compartments and almost every passenger purchased one or two packets. Roy and Das also did the same. The peanuts were really good. Both of them reached Calcutta and part company. While Roy went home, Das took a train next to Burdwan. In Burdwan he contacted shopkeepers and those who roasted peanuts. He finalised a business deal with them to send a pack of 25 kg of roasted peanuts to his Calcutta address. From third day Das started his business and was selling packets of roasted peanuts in Calcutta. There was almost no time gap between identification of opportunity and setting up an enterprise based on the same. As soon as an opportunity is felt, mind of an would-be-entrepreneur starts visualising when to establish, what kind of factory shed to be constructed, etc. The ability to visualize is called simulation. Of course mere simulation is not enough without a sound backing of costing, accounting, abilities and skills. The point here emphasized is to understand how an opportunity is transformed into a business. Opportunities manifest themselves in a number of ways but grabbing the best one is the brightest quality of entrepreneurship.

4.9 MOTIVATIONAL PATTERN WITHIN ORGANIZATION

Motivation is the desire or urge within an individual which prompts him to action. Every individual has needs, desires and drives which is termed as motives and which channelise all his behaviour and action towards achievement of some objectives. A great deal of research has been done in this area and there are many theories on motivation. But here the subject of motivation covers various motivational factors that lead to varying degrees of motivation not the theories as such. Katz and Kahn in their book Social Psychology of Organisation have defined four basic motive patterns. These four basic motive patterns can produce the required behavior in organisation are:

1. Legal compliance – the pattern is evoked by the use of unambiguous symbols of authority. It tends to produce performance at the minimum acceptable level under fear for punishment.
2. Instrumental satisfaction – the pattern is evoked by the use of rewards. Individual rewards can lead to high motivation.
3. Self-expressions – the motive pattern depends on the objective attributes of the job itself. As the job increases responsibility, the individual has an increased chance to use his own skills and abilities and through performance of the job, can derive more satisfaction and increased motivation. High productivity and strong attraction to the system are characteristic of this motive pattern though this does not necessarily imply that the individual will be highly motivated to perform for the organisation. He probably will be highly motivated to perform the job well because of the intrinsic aspect of the job.
4. Internalization of organisational goal – this motive pattern may be the most effective but also is the most difficult to evoke. The extent of the internalization of organisational goal depend on the nature of the goals and degree to which they are constant with the needs and values of the individual. It depends also on the extent to which the individual is autonomous and has control over his destiny through participation in the determination of organisational decisions and reward, which comes through organisation. This motive pattern should lead to extremely low turn over, high motivation and spontaneity and creatively in order to reach the organisational goal. Factors which lead to motivation – (*a*) Intrinsic job factor. Maslow's hierarchy needs on a five level order states that higher order needs do not become important until the lower order needs are relatively well satisfied. The needs going from the lower order to higher order are as follows:

   (*a*) Basic psychological needs, such as, hunger
   (*b*) Safety needs
   (*c*) Social needs
   (*d*) Esteem and self-realizations
   (*e*) The needs for realization and accomplishment.

Much research has been done which referred to the applicability of the needs hierarchy to the industrial environment. Two of the major studies that indicate the importance of the higher order needs are the Hawthorne studies and the Herzberg studies. Herzberg found that when they said they felt good about their jobs where factors that were genuine motivators and these invariably had to do with accomplishments, feeling of growth, job interest and job responsibilities. What made these men feel good was clearly related to self-actualization or the higher order needs Maslow specified which were also directly associated with feelings of being motivated.

The managerial strategy, if Maslow's assumptions are true, might imply different things. When higher order needs are relevant, perhaps manager should be less concerned about being considerate and friendly and more concerned with how to make work more challenging and meaningful. Perhaps emphasis should be on giving people more autonomy and responsibility and moving them along in terms of reorganisational advancement for positive achievements on the job.

Role of money in organisational motivation – it has been established by long experience and substantial evidence that in most cases when an incentive system is installed, productivity increases. One of the most neglected finding of Hawthorne studies was that the preferred incentive system was one of the key factors in the increased productivity.

Recently there have been basically two lines of thinking with regard to the role of money motivations. The first of these is called "expectancy theory" and the other is the "concept of equity". Under expectancy theory people expect that money will follow effective performance. If money has a positive value for an individual, higher performance will follow. Results of studies conducted were simple, straight forward and unequivocal that money was a powerful tool in increasing motivation. The concept of equity involves a concept of "fairplay". Most people have subjective fillings of what is fair and will be highly motivated to work. Performance is to match an estimate of a fair day's work for a fair day's pay.

However, money is the most commonly used motivating factor in the form of salary, bonus, incentives, communications and rewards. Salary or wage is of course the primary motivation and poorer the economic background of an individual, the greater the motivation of value of money. But man does not live by bread alone. Man is a social animal and seeks recognition and status in society. The status or position which an individual enjoys in the organisation, the number of people work under him, the non-monetary benefits and perks are more important than the actual take home pay packet. More over individuals are motivated by different benefit at different stage of life. As one moves up to important position, the importance of money as motivating factor decreases and intangible factors, such as, job satisfaction, confidence of the boss, good relationship with colleagues, respect commanded in the organisation etc., become more important.

The physical environment in which an individual work also has a tremendous motivational force. The design and content of actual work is in itself an important motivational factor. Freedom to take decisions and assume responsibility for the results are factors which enhance an individual's self confidence and feeling self-esteem. The more such factors can be built in job, the greater would be the job satisfaction of the individual performing the job.

Much research has also been conducted to answer the question – what makes an effective leader? This is because a good manager being a good leader can motivate people coming from diverse and different background and working in different levels. The manager's or the leader's job is to understand the motivational factors and design the work, rewards, work environment, work relationship. The manager or the leader is not only to motivate the people but also provide leadership to his men. He is to inspirer and influence subordinates to willingly work towards achieving the organisational objective.

4.10 PROBLEM WHILE GROWING-UP

Even having all the facilities & knowledges in hand to develop a small enterprise, problem do arise as bolts from blue to thwart its growth. Many of them are complex and confusing. Qualitative growth is the significant sign of healthy enterprise but growth in itself brings problems in its wake. Healthy growth must be a directed growth. If growth just happens, there is a chance of lopsided one and the feature is in danger.

The growth of an enterprise depends on leadership without which resources of production remain resources and never become production. In a competitive economy, the quality and performance of the managers determine the success of a business and ultimately its survival. Management is a universal in the modern industrial world. The chief function of a manager is the integration and application of the knowledge and analytical approaches developed by numerous disciplines. Managers problem is to seek a balance among these approaches and apply the pertinent concepts in specific situations which require action. There are three basic concepts of management:

1. An economic recourse as one of the factors of production together with land, labour and capital. The managerial resources of enterprise determine its productivity and profitability.
2. Management is a system of authority. The emergence of constitutional management characterised by a concern for definite and consistent policies and procedures for dealing with the working group.
3. Management is a class and status system. The complexity of relationship in modern society demands that managers become an elite of brains and education.

Keeping in view the above concepts, a growing enterprise needs the application of scientific management. The working force of any enterprise is vital because their expectations and their performances defined on fulfillment of their expectations besides other internal pressures, the demands from customers, and the Govt. rules and procedures, various environmental factors arising out of social needs. In a growing stage innumerable problems mentioned above do affair before the management. These expectations demand higher managerial excellence and social responsibility. A growing enterprise need managers with scientific, reasonable ad strong working senses to overcome all these teething troubles arising out of expectations from different directions.

As the business grows, situations demand changes. Managers are to measure up these changed demands to survive. It has to concede to the expectations of the people concerned and just its values and ways to suit the changed and the changing demands of society. This is not easy and this does not happen. The readjustments have to be brought and accepted consciously. While growing, workforces do not grow automatically. They have to be grown. This is one of the most vital factors for any enterprise to develop, train up and motivate the workforce to rise to the occasion to buildup a healthy organisation.

A growing enterprise has to operate and to regulate its affairs according to societal needs and environment. The manager should constantly remember that he has no right to alienate from society at large by their thoughtlessness or shortsighted actions. This raises the question of business effects. It may be an idea with some of the unscrupulous businessmen that business need have nothing to do with ethics and that all is fair in love and war. This attitude may prove deadly in terms of the future business system as a whole. The right slogans should be:

1. All decision and actions of an enterprise should be based on "Acceptance not compulsion".
2. All entrepeneural actions should be based on the principle of reason and not on force.
3. The principle of leadership by objective goals and by integration of voluntary efforts into cooperative teamwork rather than leadership by command or fear should be followed.
4. The principles of social ethics not the principles of materialism only will help to survive.
5. Leadership based on social values are practicable. If it is based on any other bases, it may mislead and bring disaster.

5

Management for Small Enterprises

5.1 BASIC MANAGEMENT PRINCIPLES

An entrepreneur is to form the duty of a manager in a small enterprise. While initially establishing an enterprise, he is to function as an enterprise, he is to function as an entrepreneur but in the operational stage, he is expected to perform the role of a manager because effective management capabilities are the key factors to bring success. Major management tasks are:

1. *Planning* : It involves setting up a line of action such as marketing resource management, profit generation etc. It involves formulation of policies and strategies to implement the plan, which must specify what is aimed at and how to achieve it. As a manager he anticipates the future and discover alternative course of action with the help of tactical and strategic policies. He is involved in decision making the process by which a course of action in consciously chosen from available alternatives for the purchase of achieving desired result.
2. *Organizing* : Entrepreneurs will have to organize their efforts and activities, organizing is a process by which the structure and allocation of jobs is determined. The employer-employee relationship, are to be established for maintaining higher worker productivity for economic goal and survival of the unit.
3. *Coordinating* : Coordination of physical resources needed at various stages like procurement of raw materials and consumables, managing financial resources, productive use of labour and application of appropriate marketing strategies etc., should be done very carefully. An entrepreneur at the helm of the enterprise is expected to function as a coordinator to bring positive results by utilizing whatever resources are in his possession by maximum utilization of the same.
4. *Controlling* : It means the process that measures current performance and guides it towards some predetermined goal. Controlling involves systematic efforts to set

performance and to keep periodical track of actual performance. It helps to check the cost and wastages in any form resulting from any point within the organization.

5. *Leading and Motivating* : Motivating them for productive purpose and efficient performance should be his vital quality. While performing the job of a manager an entrepreneur requires managerial skills, problem solving skill and a sense of time management. The entrepreneur will have to interact with many people and in diverse situation and will have to make right decision. Basically an entrepreneur must possess three fundamental skills:

   (*a*) Conceptual Skills
   (*b*) Human Relations Skills
   (*c*) Technical Skills

6. *Decision Making* : Decision making is a process of action consciously chosen from available alternatives for the purpose of achieving a desired result. A decision involves a choice. If there is but one alternative, no decision is possible. A decision involves mental process at conscious level. The logical aspects are important. A decision is purposive. It is made to facilitate the attainment of some objectives desired for benefit of the unit.

   However, decision making process maybe described in five steps:

   1. A good decision maker must be consciously aware of the factors that set the stage for decision. Past actions and decisions provide the structure for current decisions. The decision maker must recognize that he can not consider all the facts and that he must develop a selective approach for keeping the most important and relevant facts in mind. In this stage creative ability is put to test. The decision maker is to try to dig out to increase the probabilities. What is needed is an attempt to lay a good foundation for understanding the situation.
   2. A good decision is dependent on the recognition of the right problem. The key duties of the decision maker will be: to search for problems, out of the maze of problems and facts, the decision maker will have to frame his understanding of the problem and search for the correct question of decision making determining the end to be sought. A decision is rational if it selects means that lead to the desired end. It is useful to try to differentiate between means and ends. In reality an end for one decision is a means for another. The continuous process to be viewed as a means end chain.
   3. Search and analysis of available alternatives and their probable consequences is the step most subject to logical and systematic treatment. The approach of logic is the key to this step. Goals can be ranked by the decision maker and included in the conscious determination of alternatives and consequences.
   4. Even in the best-designed frame-work of alternative consequences, the crucial step remains the selection of the solution. At this stage ranking of preferences is important. The best decision may be better in degrees than a number of satisfactory ones. But the best is the best in itself.
   5. A decision must be acceptable to the unit. The decision must be communicated to the people concerned and they must be motivated to implement the decision.

Summing up the process

1. Fact-finding, investigation and collecting information.
2. To avoid appearances of arbitrary decisions, try to secure support for a right position.
3. To make a decision a choice among the alternatives.
4. To select among alternative solutions the best one.
5. Motivate people concerned to accept the selected decision for better results.

Management by Objective (MBO)

Good management must develop a way in which objectives can be used to focus attention of individual members of the organization that are meaningful to them. Objectives so drawn should be discussed among the key persons of every area where performance and results directly and vitally affect the survival and prosperity of the enterprise. Each executive must narrow the range of attention of each person in the organization to focus on definite and measurable results that have clear meaning for each individual. Each department can contribute toward organizational objectives if it clearly sees its own specific goals. Objectives must be realistic. It should be stated in definite terms of results. Clearly defined objectives lay the foundation for the performance of an organization. It should be kept in mind that the objectives so carefully quantified must be practical, technically feasible and attainable and it also must be time bound to bring results as set.

5.2 MARKETING MANAGEMENT

After a product is manufactured, the question arises, how the produce is to reach consumer? The route can be very simple or complex depending on:

(*a*) Nature of the product
(*b*) Location of the market
(*c*) Price of the product
(*d*) The availability of middlemen willing to handle it
(*e*) The sales effort required
(*f*) The resources and capabilities of the produce

The channel management depends on:

1. Terms of contract
2. Relationship with the middlemen and their cooperation
3. Sufficient assistances are provided by the manufacturer to enable middlemen to market the products successfully.

Marketing covers:

(*a*) Pre-Selling (Product Selling, Market Research, Marketing Plan formulations)
(*b*) Selling (Product Introduction, negotiation, closing sales)
(*c*) Post-Selling activities (After sales service, spare-parts supply, warranty and guarantees)

An entrepreneur must very deeply understand that the effectiveness of the marketing effort of any product depends on the decisions made in each of the 4Ps of marketing and their effective combination to meet the needs of the consumer. The combination of the 4Ps which are also known as Marketing Mix are:

(*a*) Product
(*b*) Price
(*c*) Place
(*d*) Promotion

(a) Product

(*i*) Package/Brand Name
(*ii*) Additional features: size, colour, style, model etc.
(*iii*) After sales service/guarantee/warranty

(b) Price

(*i*) Same as competitors/cheaper/what will market bear
(*ii*) Cost plus overheads plus profit margin
(*iii*) High price, less discount
(*iv*) Credit terms (any secret deal)
(*v*) Buy one, get one or two free
(*vi*) Free Gifts, coupons, prizes
(*vii*) Cash Discounts

(c) Place

(*i*) Agents/wholesellers/retailers
(*ii*) Merchandising
(*iii*) Mail Order
(*iv*) Direct Selling of any aggressive type

(d) Promotion

(*i*) Display
(*ii*) Advertising
(*iii*) Publicity through sales campaign
(*iv*) Leaflets, handouts through little box, newspaper
(*v*) Telephone Selling
(*vi*) Bill-Board advertisements
(*vii*) Free sampling, gifts, coupons etc.

5.3 ADVERTISING

It is the means of informing as well as influencing the general public to buy products or services and to create awareness through visual or oral messages. It helps to create demand, promote marketing system and boast economic growth.

Different advertising media are:

(*a*) Newspaper

(*b*) Radio
(*c*) Television
(*d*) Hoardings and Neon Signs
(*e*) Taxi, Bus and Train body panels
(*f*) Bill Boards
(*g*) Cinema slides and short film ads.
(*h*) Direct mailing of literature
(*i*) Demonstrations
(*j*) Sales campaign

When sales budget is prepared, a certain amount may be fixed for this activity. An analysis of expenditures on advertising may be done annually to examine whether it was effective or not. A cost effectiveness may guide future policy of involvement in advertising.

Impact of Advertising: Advantages of advertising are:

(*a*) Increased sales
(*b*) Quick turnover
(*c*) Creating dealer interest
(*d*) Lowering costs
(*e*) Creation of goodwill
(*f*) Encourages employees for improved performance

5.4 HUMAN RELATIONS

An entrepreneur deals with people and must be able to "get along" with them. Human Relations concentrates on developing this skill of cooperation with others. Individual members of a group have their own personal ideas of what results they want to achieve. The needs of individuals are important as bases for their motivation. People will cooperate as long as the goals of a group are consistent with their ideas of their own goal. The individual has many goals. Some tend to conflict, some are more important to him than others, some are short run and some are long run.

The organizational objectives are non-personal, yet they must remain consistent with the personal objectives of individuals in the organization. If an individual is to accept organizational objectives he must feel that achieving the organizational goals will satisfy or at least not conflict with his own personal goals. Organizational goals must serve as common denominations for the entire group. Some organizational goals will conflict with the goals of the individual and he will continue to cooperate unless he becomes convinced that the conflict is fundamental.

Good human relations stimulate people to strive for overall improvement and create a healthy organizational environment, which encourages:

(*a*) High punctuality and less absenteeism
(*b*) Stimulates cooperation, avoid industrial strife and disagreement
(*c*) Boost morale and motivation

Morale: Morale is defined in many ways. In the industrial field, it reflects more group oriented concepts and group cohesion. If the workforce is generally satisfied the cost will be less.

Motivation and Money Factor

Morale and motivation are hard to treat independently. This is not because morale causes motivation rather because the same thing may result in the co-variation of the morale and motivation. Sometimes 'impact of money' as motivator is described as a powerful tool. It has been clearly established that 'incentive systems' lead to higher productivity. It is perceived that the workers performance and payments are related.

Touch and Win Magic

An entrepreneur should try to build up a congenial environment within the unit and assure smooth production to cater to the needs of the society and to achieve this purpose, he needs a close study of the organizational behaviour. He must be alert to know the organizational health of the unit by taking a deep study from time to time based on the following areas and make a patriarchal approach to build up a fraternity among workers:

(*a*) Individual needs and wants of the workforce and introduce the principle of personal touch with them.
(*b*) Behaviour of the small group, unhappy and immediate redressal.
(*c*) Behaviour of the supervisors and him to play the role of patriarch.
(*d*) Inter-group behaviour to introduce healthy competitive attitude.

This 'touch and win' magic makes a tremendous reaction among the workforce.

5.5 PROCESS OF ORGANISATIONAL CHANGE

People change their knowledge, attitude and behavior when they become dissatisfied. A successful change involves:

(*a*) Recognizing the need for it
(*b*) Learning a new behavior or substitute
(*c*) Feeling comfortable with the new situation.

Change process may be described in three stages of Unfreezing, Moving and Refreezing.

Unfreezing

Changes does not occur in a vacuum of no prior perspective. Recognising major changes in the environment and problems within organisation are the first step toward organisation change. Once the need for change is identified, it has to be communicated to people who will be involved in the changing process. The following strategies may be adopted to increase member's acceptance of a change:

(*a*) Express the need for change
(*b*) Communicate the potential benefit

(c) Protect the interest of concerned people
(d) Get people involved in the process
(e) Communicate the progress of change
(f) Utilize services of a respected change agent
(g) Reinforce earlier changes.

Most of the strategies designed to increase the driving force are equally applicable for reducing the resting force to change. People resist change because they perceive that it can be harmful to them. So it is essential that they be made aware of its needs and benefits. Understanding the reason why people resist change can help to formulate a plan to reduce the resistance.

Moving

In the moving or changing phase, the individual is ready for new behavior and a change in perspective. It is the time of trial and error learning, charaterised by ambiguity. The face is typically, one of careful guidance by an authority, of learning the new pattern of behavior before the whole can be conceived. Moving or change involves changing the organisational components. The approach is based on four major components – task, structure, technology and people. Change in any one of them requires changing the others.

Refreezing

This is the final phase. It involves the establishment of a new perspective compatible with and leading to the new desirable behavior. This is the period in which the individual or group begins to enjoy the rewards for the new behavior in the form of social approval, monitory reward or in the form of ego satisfaction and sense of self-fulfillment. In order to continuously reinforce the newly acquired behavior, the organisation needs to maintain organisational tempo among various components that are supportive of such behavior. Without such organisational compatibility, the organisation will encounter instability. Since both internal and external components change constantly, organisational tempo cannot exist at one level for a longtime. Thus the task of performing organisational change becomes a continuous process. The success stories of change have taught that the organisational changes are typically initiated at the top management level. There may be distressing symptoms. So a lot of unfreezing interventions are required at the top. This is the typical trial and error changing process and search for results continues. Only when enough reinforcements are received from positive results, a change is established. The three stages of organisational change process – unfreezing, moving and refreezing are always to be achieved through adaptation, avoidance and control.

5.6 DEVELOPMENT OF INTERPERSONAL SKILLS

The development of interpersonal skills can be continued to four stages:

(a) Forming fist impression
(b) Developing mutual expectation
(c) Honoring Psychological contracts
(d) Developing trust and influence.

The process is not inborn. In order to develop a close and binding relationship people must expose themselves to each other. Unless they know each other well, they cannot develop a trusting relationship.

The Johari window is a conceptual model for studying interpersonal awareness. It was developed by Joseph Luft and Harry Ingham. It is a schematic model that shows how people expose themselves to others and receive feedback from others in their interpersonal relationships. The Johari window has four compartments – Arena, Blindspot, Closed and Dark. Arena represents the 'public self' that is known to the self, but not to others. The Dark area is neither known to the self nor to others.

JOHARI AWARENESS MODEL OF INTERPERSONAL PROCESS

	Known to self	Unknown to self
known to others	ARENA (Shared and mutually held public information, feelings and motives)	BLIND SPOT (Information, feelings reactions etc. known only to others.)
unknown to others	CLOSED (Hidden information motives feelings etc. known only to the self)	DARK (Undiscovered potentials & creative reservoir known neither to self nor others)

The implication of this model is that if Arena is small, there is little free and spontaneous interaction. The larger the arena, the greater the chance for participation in any relationship to make correct perceptual judgments about each other. As Arena expands, the closed area or private self shrinks. The Blind spot takes longer to reduce because self-concept protection mechanisms are involved. Arena can be expanded by mean of self-discloser and feedback. Self-discloser means revealing oneself to another person and sharing one's feelings, emotions, facts and knowledge with that individual. Self-discloser involves both rewards and costs. Being open offers the possibility of self-understanding, growth and better interpersonal adjustments. On the other hand, discloser takes the risk of being rejected, misinterpreted. However unless some one takes the risk and initiates self-discloser, the relationship will not develop.

Feedback reduces Blind Spot and help us to increase our self-awareness. We can guess how they see us by their reactions but these reactions are often not clear and likely to be misperceived. Unless we received feedback as to how they see us or what kind of effects our behaviours have on them, we are likely to be blind to their feelings and relations.

Interpersonal awareness can be increased in several ways. When you feel some thing is wrong with a relationship but the problem area cannot be identified. Nothing really happens in a relationship until the participants learn to trust each other. But trusting another person is not so simple because it involves risk of being exploited or taken for granted. If the other person behaves in such a manner that violates one's trust, the relationship cannot continue. There are few things a person can do to create and maintain a trusting relationship:

(*a*) Take the initiative in self-discloser. This can set the tone for developing and maintaining a relationship of trust.

(*b*) Accept another person's self-discloser. Appreciate the other person for taking the initiative and the risk of rejection.

(*c*) Reciprocate another's initiative with your own self-discloser. Failure to do so will be interpreted by the other person as a lack of interest and will arouse the anxiety of possible exploitation. It is to be kept in mind that the self-fulfilling prophecy works in an interpersonal relationship. If you assume that the other person cannot be trusted, you will find evidence to that effect. If you assume that other person can be trusted, you are likely to experience the same.

5.7 LEADERSHIP STYLES

Leadership is the activity of influencing people to strive willingly for group activities. The different leadership styles are:

(*a*) Human relations style,
(*b*) Theory of 'X' and 'Y' style,
(*c*) Authoritarian, Democratic and Laissez-faire style,
(*d*) Employee-oriented style,
(*e*) Production-orientation style,
(*f*) Consideration and Initiating structure style,
(*g*) Scientific Management style.

Styles have been related to various theories of leadership such as, Trait theory, Group and Exchange theory, Social Learning theory, Managerial Grid theory, Contingency theory and Path-goal theory. In the context of leadership and influence process, a distinction is drawn between authority and power. Power is divided into five types, such as, legitimate power, reward power, expect power, charismatic power and coercive power. Based on these types of power there may be two types of leaders:

(1) Formal and
(2) Informal.

The word style is the way in which the leader influences the followers. There various studies that helps to understand the leadership styles.

1. Hawthorne studies – ELTON MAOY and Roethllsberger did a series of studies from 1924 to 1932 in an electricity company at Illinois in U.S.A. There studies are known as Hawthorne studies. The study initially aimed at finding out if changes in illumination, rest periods and lunch breaks can affect the productivity of workers. It was found that less light, shorter and fewer rest periods and shorter lunch break resulted in an increase in productivity. Once all these changes were eliminated and the normal working conditions were resumed, it was also seen that the worker's productivity and the feeling of being together went up. The increase in productivity was attributed to the attitude of workers towards each other and their feeling of togetherness. Attention paid to the workers by the researchers made them feel important which resulted in improvement in their work performance. This is known as Hawthorne effect. A good leader aught to keep the above aspects in his style of workup with people and supervising their work.

2. Theory of X & Y – Mc Gregor categorised leadership style in two broad categories. The theory X style of leaders believe that most people dislike work and will avoid it where possible. This style of leadership exercises strong control and direction and wherever necessary punish people if they do not do the work. If people do the work as desired, they may even get monitory and other rewards. Theory of Y leaders assume that people will work hard and assume responsibility if they can satisfy personal needs of goals of their organisation. Search leaders do not distinguish between the leaders and the follower in contract to theory X style. They feel that people control themselves within rather than being controlled by other such as a leader or a manager or a supervisor. An effective leader needs to examine carefully his own idea about the motivation and behavior of subordinates and others as well as the situation before adopting a particular style of leadership.
3. Michigan Study – Likert of university of Michigan Survey Research Centre identified two major styles of leadership orientations – (*a*) employees orientation & (*b*) production orientation. The employee oriented style of leader emphasises the relation ship aspect of the jobs of the individuals. Such leaders take interest in or everyone and accept the individuality and personal needs of the individual. He has complete confidence and trust in all matters in his subordinates. His subordinates feel free to discuss things about their jobs with their superior. The effective leaders always ask subordinates for ideas and opinions and always tries to make constructive use of them. Likert showed that the employee oriented style brought high-producing performance compared with prudential oriented style.
4. Scientific Manager's Style – Taylor emphasised the importance of having management and labour work in harmony to maximise profits. The best way to increase output was to improve the techniques or methods used by workers. Therefore profit can be maximized by using systematic and scientifically based approach to study jobs. According to the scientific managerial style, Management of a work organisation must be divorced from human affairs and emotions and people have to adjust to the management and not management to the people. The leader is assumed to be the most competent individual in planning and organising the work of subordinates according to Taylor's principle of scientific management.
5. Democratic Leadership Style – Lewin did a study on three different styles of leadership. The authoritarian was very directive and did not allow any participation. The democratic leader encouraged discussion with the group and allowed participation in making decision. The Laissez-faire leader gave complete freedom and did not provide any leadership and did not establish any policies or procedures to do the task. Lewin's study was a pioneering effort in understanding leadership styles from the point of scientific methodology. He threw light on how different styles of leadership can produce different complex reactions from same or similar group.

Many theories have been suggested by the researchers regarding which leadership style is most effective. But the effectiveness of the leadership styles is also different on environment and organisational structure of the organisation.

5.8 QUANTITATIVE TECHNIQUES FOR MANAGERS

Some very important advances have been made in the quantitative disciplines-mathematics and statistics. Although most managers do not possess the necessary background to make some of the calculations that refined decision-making techniques require. It is becoming increasingly clear that managers must be able to understand the quantitative approach well enough to:

1. State their problems in forms that will facilitate the use of specialists in handling quantitative data,
2. Communicate with specialists in the interpretation of the answers obtained by refined methods.

Numerous quantitative techniques are available for managers. A checklist is given below for a firsthand knowledge.

CHECKLIST OF QUANTITATIVE TECHNIQUES

Name of Technique	*Applications*	*Description*
1. Sampling	Market research work sampling. Inventory control. Auditing	Through the use of various designs, sampling makes possible inferences about population characteristic with specified degrees of reliability.
2. Linear programming	Used to allocate scarce resources in an optimum manner in problems of scheduling, product mix and so on.	Key factors include an objective function, choice among several alternatives, limits or constraints stated in symbols, and variables assumed to be linear.
3. Decision theory	Used to select the best course of action when information is given in probabilistic form.	Developments in Bayesian statistics allow the executive's judgment to be systematically brought into the analysis of problems.
4. Correlation	The study of the degree of functional relationship among two or more variables.	One variable can be estimated if, the value of another variable is known. Key factors: regression analysis, correlation coefficients, and scatter diagrams.
5. Game theory	Used to determine the optimum strategy in a competitive situation.	Most solutions involve two persons, sum zero competitive situations (ones in which two people are involved and one person wins exactly what the other loses). More complex situations become extremely involved.

(Contd.)

Name of Technique	Applications	Description
6. Index numbers	Measurement of fluctuations in price, volume, economic activity, or other variables over a period of time, relative to a base.	Important factors include the choice of the base period, the method of weighting, and the selection of the components to be included in the index.
7. Times series analysis	Interpretation of sales, production, price, or other variable over a period of time.	Series of data over a period of time are analyzed as to their chief types of fluctuations such as trend, cyclical, Seasonal, and irregular.
8. Simulation	Used to imitate an operation or process prior to actual performance. Business games are popular applications.	Long periods of time are simulated in short trials. Complex group of variables can be handled when known mathematical method is available.
9. Waiting-line theory	To analyze the feasibility of adding facilities and to assess the amount and cost of waiting time.	Most models assume a specific distribution of arrivals and service times. Sometimes called queuing theory.
10. PERT (program evaluation review technique)	Planning and control of a complex set of activities, functions, and relationship	Key concepts include: (1) Network of events and activities; (2) Resource allocation; (3) Time and cost consideration; (4) Network paths; (5) Critical paths
11. Statistical quality control charts	To distinguish those variations due to change from those due to – assignable causes in production.	Result of sample (e.g. means and range) are plotted, on charts having upper and lower control limits. If values for the sample fall within these limits, the production process is considered under control. If outside management should look for a cause of the variations.
12. Inventory models	Determine when and how much inventory to carry.	Simple models assume no delivery delay and that demand is known. Probabilistic models handle situations of risk and uncertainty.
13. Integrated production models	Used to minimize cost with respect to workforce production, and inventory	A highly complex model, of use only to companies with detailed histories of sales and costs.

Source: Essentials of Management by J.L. Massie

5.9 NETWORK ANALYSIS*

Network analysis is a general purpose schematic technique used to identify all the interconnecting links in a system. The technique is useful for describing the elements in a complex situation for the purpose of designing, planning, co-ordinating, controlling and making decisions. The network approach has many applications; we shall discuss one which focuses on the critical path in scheduling.

Critical path analysis uses network analysis for scheduling production, construction projects, and research and development activities and in other situations that require estimates of time and performance. A sophisticated version of this technique (PERT – Program Evaluation and Review Technique) was first developed for use in defense projects, specifically in the development of the Polaris missile program, but it can be used in many scheduling situations.

The first step in network analysis, is to separate each element, or link, and describe it in terms of other elements in the system. In order to present a network pictorially, one must distinguish the activities and events involved. An activity is a *time-consuming* effort necessary to complete a particular part of the total project; it is represented by an arrow (→) that shows the direction of the sequential activities. An event is a specific *instant of time* that denotes the beginning and end of an activity; an event is represented by an ellipse or circle. An event cannot accomplished until all activities preceding it have been completed. All activities begin and end with an event. The event is a "milestone", or signal, for dependent succeeding activities to begin. Events usually are assigned numbers sequentially for identification and analysis. In thinking through the process, one must repeatedly check three questions about the events and activities: (1) which must be accomplished before a given event? (2) which cannot be accomplished until an event is completed? And (3) which can be accomplished concurrently?

After a network has been prepared and times for each activity have been noted, it is then possible to determine the path that consists of those events and activities that require the maximum time (by adding the times for all activities along the path). This path is "critical" since it identifies the sequence of activities that will determine the minimum time in which the project can be completed. The critical path requires greater attention on path will postpone the final completion date of the project. (2) Special study of each of the activities along the path may result in possible methods by which more resources or more concurrent activities or changing the technology used may reduce the time required, which in turn would reduce the overall project time. (3) Advance planning and improvements along the critical path may cause another path then to become critical. In short, the critical path approach directs management's attention to the "exceptional" and most significant facts, spots potential bottlenecks early, and avoids unnecessary pressure on the other paths that will not result in an earlier final completion date.

The Program Evaluation and Review Technique (PERT) a special application of network analysis, has received the greatest amount of attention because it has developed statistical refinements for estimating the time required for each activity and because it is of greatest help in new projects for which little past experience is available. In these cases, PERT has refined the network technique (usually with the help of electronic computers) and has provided danger signals for management that require decisions for trade-off in times required, resources allocated or quality specifications.

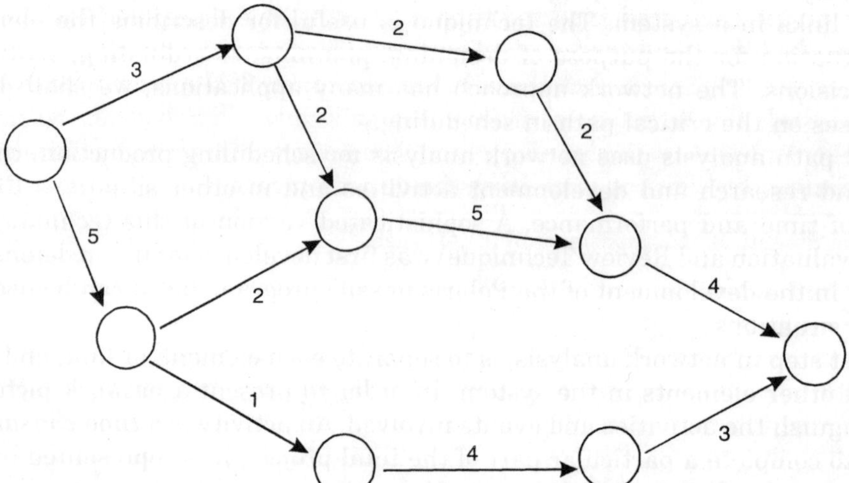

Illustration of A Skeleton Net Work and The Critical Path

In handling the times for an activity in a network, a single best estimate may not be reliable when compared with the time that the activities actually take. In order to arrive at a more reliable estimate, three time values are usually employed: the most optimistic estimate (t_p), most likely time (t_o), and the pessimistic estimate (t_p). The optimistic time is the shortest time possible if everything goes perfectly with no complications; the chance of this optimum actually occurring might be one in a hundred. The pessimistic time is the longest time conceivable; it includes time for unusual delays, and thus the chance of its happening might be what normally would occur. If only one time were used, it would be the most likely time (t_m). The difference in the three time estimates gives a measure of the relative uncertainty involved in the activity. From these times, the expected time (t_e) can be computed by applying statistical techniques. The expected time (t_e) is the weighted arithmetic mean of the times. It may or may not be the same as the most likely estimate (t_m) since the differences between the optimistic and most likely and the pessimistic and most likely would not necessarily by equal. The calculation of t_e is based on a statistical distribution of probabilities and can become quite complicated. However it has been found that the formula

$$t_e = \frac{t_0 + 4t_m + t_p}{6}$$

provides approximate results that are usable. The t_e provides the time in which there is a 50-50 chance of the project being completed. The time required for each activity is shown on the arrow representing the activity; at times, it may be desirable to record t_o, t_m, and t_p, in which case the numbers are noted in that order along the arrow representing the activity.

A primary reason to estimate more than one time for an activity is to provide data by which management may determine the probabilities that each activity will be completed in a certain time. Moreover, most projects are assigned target dates, which may or may not be the same as the computed expected time (t_e) for the entire project. Slack is the difference between the target and the length of any path. Slack may be positive or negative, and it does not necessarily mean that there is time to spare. If the critical path has a time length that equals the target time, other paths will have positive slack. With these concepts, management has available information for making decisions for a variety of actions that will improve the chances of meeting the desired target.

---

*Adapted from Essentials of Management by J.L. Massie.

6

Taxation, Industrial Laws and Commercial Laws for Small Enterprises

6.1 TAXATION

6.1.1 Income Tax

The financial year of the central government is from 1st April to 31st March and the taxes are to be paid for each assessment year on the income of the previous year relevant to it. The income tax rates vary from year to year. The important points that an entrepreneur has to keep in mind are:

1. Accounting year: An entrepreneur has the freedom to choose the accounting year ending in any month of the calendar year.
2. Legal Status: Legal Status of the assessed is classified as:
   (*a*) Individual
   (*b*) Hindu undivided family
   (*c*) Company
   (*d*) Partnership firm
   (*e*) Association of persons
3. Tax Variation: Various kinds of exemptions, deductions and incentives to reduce tax burden.
4. Computation of Business Income: Aggregation of income computed under different heads after adjusting for losses, allowing deductions and tax relief result into total taxable income. The following deductions are expressly allowed in computing business income:

   (*a*) Rent, taxes, repairs and insurance of buildings used for business purpose.

(*b*) Current repairs, insurance of machinery, plant and furniture used for business purpose
(*c*) Depreciation of buildings, machinery, plant and furniture owned by the enterprise.
(*d*) Investment allowances in respect of plant and machinery.
(*e*) Expenditure on scientific research.
(*f*) Expenditure on patent and copyrights.
(*g*) Insurance premium against risk of damage.
(*h*) Bonus and commission to employees.
(*i*) Interest on borrowed capital.
(*j*) Contribution to provident fund.
(*k*) Bad debt written off.
(*l*) Amortization of preliminary expenses.

5. Deductions: Deductions are allowed from gross total income in order to determine total taxable income. Deductions are of two kinds:

(*a*) In respect of payments
(*b*) In respect of income

Deductions in respect of payments

(*a*) Life Insurance premiums, contribution of provident fund
(*b*) Donations to Charitable Institutions
(*c*) Medical expenses of handicapped dependents
(*d*) House rent paid
(*e*) Donations for scientific research or rural development

Deduction allowed in respect of Income

(*a*) Dividend and bank interest.
(*b*) Long-term capital gain in case of non-company assesses.
(*c*) 20% of profit of new industries undertaking established.
(*d*) 20% of the profits of new small-scale industries established after 30.9.1977 in certain rural areas for 10 assessment years.
(*e*) 50% of profits on export turnover plus 4% of the net foreign exchange realization.
(*f*) 25% of profit relating to execution of foreign projects.

6. Taxpayer's Obligation:

(*a*) Maintenance of accounts book with correct compensation of income. The accounts books are to be retained for a certain number of years.
(*b*) Obtaining Permanent Account (P.A.) Number. Any person whose business turnover exceeds Rs. 50,000 must apply in form no. 49A for allotment of P.A. Number.
(*c*) Filing income tax return in prescribed form will have to be filed on or before 30th June each year to the Income Tax Office.
(*d*) Payment of Tax: Taxes are to be paid within due dates.

6.1.2 Excise Duty

Excise is a tax levied by the Central Government. The tax is applied on the clearance of goods from the factory. The rate of excise depends on the items manufactured and these rates vary as per the decisions of the Government. The penalties under the Excise Act for non-compliance are very severe and can create a lot of difficulties for the enterprise.

Excise Rules

(*a*) In order to encourage small scale Industries, the central government has introduced a policy of not levying any excise duty up to a specific value of the clearance. This excise free limit again is changed from time to time. The entrepreneur is to ascertain whether his product attracts excise duty.

(*b*) Excise duty has to be paid at a specific rate. It may be in Rupee per Kg or a specific percentage of value of unit of the goods cleared. It requires to be ascertained at what rate the excise duty is payable.

(*c*) In order to avoid cumulative effect of excise, the central government gives set off on the purchase made by enterprise, if an excise duty has been paid by the supplier. The entrepreneur should find out the amount set off and conditions to be satisfied for availing of the set off.

(*d*) Whenever a business subject to excise levy, certain formalities like getting the license, maintenance of the clearance records, system of the Gate Pass, etc., are to be observed. The entrepreneur should follow these laid down procedures to avoid legal action.

In view of the complexity of the excise rules, the entrepreneur must see the concerned official in the excise department or to consult who is well aware of the excise rules.

6.1.3 Sales Tax

Sales Tax is a state levy. It is charged whenever the goods are purchased from within the state. The 'Central Sales Tax' is levied when the goods are purchased from outside of the state. The seller charges the sales tax from the buyer and hands it over to the government. As such it has been made obligatory for the firm having a turnover exceeding specific limit to get the sales tax registration. It is optional for the firm to get the registration for the Central Sales Tax. Any enterprise having registration is known as Registered Dealers, whereas unregistered units are known as Unregistered Dealers.

Procedures to be followed in connection with Sales Tax

It means registration of the unit under the sales tax law. The entrepreneur is to contact the sales tax department in the state. Application in prescribed form along with copies of the partnership deed, proof of permanent place of business, registration under Shop Act or rent receipt or Municipal tax bill is to be submitted to them. Normally no fee is charged. The sales tax department will give registration number bearing Sales Tax number.

Filing of Return

After having registered, the entrepreneur is to maintain the books of accounts and submit periodical returns to the sales tax authorities. Returns is a statement of figures showing all sales and purchases with all claims such as tax free goods, goods sold against certain forms required under ACT and also showing taxable balance and the amount of tax payable.

Payment of Tax

The tax payable must be deposited in government treasury or through authorized banks in the prescribed form known as 'Challan'. Return and Challan should be submitted together in a prescribed time.

Benefits

Sales tax related concessions of benefits are awarded to attract certain class of manufacturers by different state governments. Sometimes, schemes of sales tax loan are offered. Some states have introduced deferred payment scheme. For the betterment of the backward areas, tax free zone is also declared.

6.2 INDUSTRIAL LAWS

6.2.1 Factories Act-1948

The act is intended to ensure health, safety and welfare of workers in factories. The act purposes to ensure the above by making provisions for:

(*a*) Licensing for factories
(*b*) Minimum requirement with regard to cleanliness, disposal of wastages and effluents, dust and fume, over crowding, lighting etc.
(*c*) Hours of work, rest intervals, spread-over, weekly holidays.
(*d*) Restoring the employment of women and children in certain occupations and at certain times.
(*e*) Leave with wages.
(*f*) Extra payment, overtime allowance if the prescribed hours are exceeded.
(*g*) Notice in the case of accidents, dangerous occurrences and diseases etc.

Safety and Protection

Children and women cannot be employed in occupations, which are deemed dangerous. For providing safety against dangerous and moving parts of the machines, this Act requires the factory owners to make suitable arrangements for fencing, covering or guarding the machines. Safety devises are to be supplied to workers and remedial measures are to be brought within their knowledge for protecting them against fire, dangerous fumes, inflammable materials and occupational diseases.

6.2.2 Workmen's Compensation Act-1923

This act provides for payment of compensation by employers to workmen and their dependents in case of personal injury caused by accident arising out of and in course of employment and for death or disablement as a result of contracting certain occupational diseases. The amount of compensation payable to dependents depends on the nature of injury, wage and age of workers. It also provides for cheaper and quicker disposal of deposits relating to compensation through special tribunals than that possible under the civil law.

6.2.3 Industrial Disputes Act-1947

The Industrial Disputes Act was enacted to make provision for the investigation and settlement of industrial disputes and for certain other purpose.

Definitions of the Terms used in the Act

(*a*) *Appropriate Government*: It means the Central Government in relation to any industrial dispute concerning any industry carried on by or under the authority of the central government. In relation to any other industrial dispute, the appropriate government is the state government.

(*b*) *Average Pay*: It means the average of the wages payable to a workman:

- (*i*) In the case of monthly paid workman in the three complete calendar months.
- (*ii*) In the case of weekly paid workmen, in the four complete work.
- (*iii*) In the case of daily paid workmen in the twelve full working days.

(*c*) *Award*: It means an interim or a final determination of any industrial dispute by any labour court, Industrial Tribunal or National Industrial Tribunal and Arbitration.

(*d*) *Industrial Dispute*: It means any dispute or difference between employers and employees or between employers and workmen or between workmen and workmen, which is connected with the employment or non-employment or the term of employment or with the conditions of labour of any reason.

(*e*) *Lay Off*: Lay off means the failure, refusal or inability of employer on account of shortage of coal, water, power or raw material of the accumulation of stocks or the breakdown of machinery or for any other reason to give employment to a workman whose name is borne on the master rolls of his industrial establishment and who has not been trenched.

(*f*) *Lock Out*: It means the temporary closing of a place of employment or the suspension of work or the refusal by an employer to continue to employ any number of persons employed by him.

(*g*) *Strike*: Strike means cessation of work by a body of persons employed in any industry acting in combination or a concerted refusal to continue to work or to accept employment.

Authorities under the Act

The appropriate government may, by general or special order, or by notification in the official gazette, constitute the following committees/awards/courts/tribunals for promoting the settlement of industrial disputes:

(*a*) Works committee
(*b*) Concilliation Officer
(*c*) Board of Concilliation
(*d*) Courts of enquiry

(*e*) Labour Courts
(*f*) Industrial Tribunals
(*g*) National Tribunals

Machinary to Settle Disputes

The authorities under the Act take necessary steps to see that any dispute between the workers and the employers are settled amicably. The government has constituted tripartite conference for various industries for the purpose of solving outstanding questions in a spirit of give and take.

Works Committee: In any industry where 100 or more workers are engaged, a works committee is constituted. The committee will consist of equal representatives of workers and employees. The main purpose of the committee is to promote measures for security and preserving good relation between the workmen and employers.

Concilliation Officers and Boards: The Industrial Disputes Act 1947 seeks to resolve disputes by conciliation. The conciliation officer or the conciliation board is empowered to take appropriate steps to bring the parties together and help them to settle their disputes amicably. The appropriate government may refer the dispute to a labour court or an Industrial Tribunal for adjudication only when no settlement is reached by conciliation.

Three Tier Adjudication Machinery

The Industrial disputes Act 1947 as amended up in 1957, provides a three tier machinery for adjudication of industrial disputes.

1. *Labour Courts*: These are constituted so that points of dispute can be discussed and verdict obtained. Important matters which can be taken up with the labour court are:
   (*a*) The legality of an order passed by an employer.
   (*b*) The application and interpretation of standing order.
   (*c*) Discharge or dismissal of workmen.
   (*d*) Withdrawal of any concession or privilege.
   (*e*) Illegality or otherwise of a strike or lockout.
2. *Industrial Tribunal*: An Industrial Tribunal is constituted either by a present or by a previous high court judge. In addition, two assessors may also be taken up by an Industrial Tribunal are:
   (*a*) Wages
   (*b*) Compensatory or other allowances
   (*c*) Hours of work and rest intervals
   (*d*) Leave and wages
   (*e*) Bonus, provident fund and gratuity
   (*f*) Shift working
   (*g*) Retrenchment of workers
3. *National Tribunal*: A national tribunal is constituted when the industrial dispute involves questions of national interest and importance or is of such a nature that

establishments situated in more than one state are likely to be interested in or affected by such a dispute. An independent person or a judge of a high court is generally appointed in the National Tribunal.

Arbitration: Arbitration can also be restored to for settling disputes on the agreement of the parties concerned who appoint an arbitrator for the purpose. The arbitration award is building upon the parties who referred the dispute to arbitration.

6.2.4 Employees State Insurance Act-1948

The broad scheme of the act is to provide for medical attendance in case of sickness, maternity and employment injury and also to provide for some cash benefits during the period of these contingencies for this purpose, a certain amount of contribution is taken from the employees and certain amount from the employers. The state government also contributes $1/8^{th}$ of share towards the cost of medical care. The employees state insurance corporation a statutory body consisting of representatives of employees, employers, medical profession, central government, state government and parliament administers the scheme, through a standing committee constituted from among the members of the corporation. This committee acts as the executive body. There is also Medical Benefit Council to advise the corporation on the matters connected with the provision of medical care.

6.2.5 The Payment of Bonus Act-1948

The act applies to every factory and every other establishment in which twenty or more persons are employed on any day during an accounting year. As per provision of the act, 'employee' means any person (other than an apprentice) employed on a salary or wage not exceeding one thousand and six hundred rupees per month in any industry to do any skilled or unskilled, manual, supervisory, managerial, administrative, technical or clerical work for hire or reward, whether the terms of emolument be expressed or implied.

Eligibility for Bonus

In accordance with the previous of the act, every employee shall be entitled to be paid by his employer in an accounting year, bonus, provided he has worked in the establishment for not less than thirty days in that year. An employee shall be disqualified from receiving bonus under this act, if he is dismissed from service for: (a) Fraud (b) Riots (c) Theft, misappropriation or shortage of any property of the establishment.

Amount of Bonus

Every employer shall be bound to pay every employee a minimum bonus which shall be 8.33 percent of the salary or wage earned by the employee during the accounting year or one hundred rupees whichever is higher, whether or not the employer has any allocable surplus in accounting year. The maximum limit of the bonus should be fixed to 20% of the total annual earnings of the workers. The quantum of bonus payable to employees drawing more than Rs. 750 will be the same as for those drawing Rs 750 per month. The bonus must be paid in cash by the employer within a period of 8 months after the close of the year. Employees employed in any establishment are debarred from entering into agreement with their employer for granting them an amount of bonus under a formula, which is different from that under the act.

6.3 COMMERCIAL LAWS

6.3.1 Indian Contracts Act-1872

Definition of Contract: A Contract is an agreement made between two or more persons, which is intended to be and is enforceable at law. It is constituted by the acceptance by one party of an offer (proposal) made to him by the other party to do or to abstain from doing an act. An offer (proposal) when accepted is called a promise and the term 'contract' denotes legal obligation which is thereby created, on the one part to perform the promise and on the other to accept the performance of it.

Offer and Acceptance: The communication of an offer (proposal) is considered complete when it comes to the knowledge of the person to whom it is made. A mere proposal not communicated by words or conduct cannot create a binding contract.

Essentials of Valid Contract

(*a*) There must be a valid agreement i.e., there must be an offer and acceptance
(*b*) The parties must be adults having sound mind
(*c*) The contract must be made by free consent of the parties and must not have agreed under:
  (*i*) Coercion
  (*ii*) Undue influence
  (*iii*) Fraud
  (*iv*) Misinterpretation
  (*v*) Mistake
(*d*) The agreement must be for a legal purpose and with a lawful object.

Performance of Contracts: The parties to a contract must either perform or offer to perform their respective promises unless such performance is dispensed with or excused under the provision of this Act or any other law.

Offer of Performance: When one part to contract offers to perform his part of it, it is for the other to accept the same. If the offer is not accepted promisor is not responsible and does not lose his right under the contract.

Modes of Discharge of Contract

(*a*) By mutual agreement, i.e., by the same way it was formed.
(*b*) By performance
(*c*) By impossibility: When parties can not fulfill their obligation under certain circumstances
(*d*) By operation of law; for example bankruptcy.

Indemnity and Guarantee

Definition of contract of indemnity: a contract by which one party promises to save the other from loss caused to him by the contract of the promisor himself or by the conduct of any other person is called a 'Contract of Indemnity'. Rights of indemnity holder: The promise or indemnity holder is entitled to recover from the promisor, all costs including damages by legal suit.

Definition of Guarantee

A 'Contract of Guarantee' is a contract to perform the promise or discharge the liability of a third person in case of his default.

In a contract of guarantee, the person he gives the guarantee is called the 'surety'. The person in respect of whose default the guarantee is given is called the 'Principal Debtor' and the person to whom the guarantee is given is called the 'creditor'. A guarantee may be either oral or written.

Surety's Liability

The liability of a surety is joint with that of the principal debtor and surety's liability would arise when the principal debtor fail to perform his obligation. The surety is liable to pay the due amount to the creditor including interest and charges which might have become due on it.

Definition of Bailment

A bailment is the delivery of goods by one person to another for some purpose upon a contract that they shall, when the purpose is accomplished, be returned or otherwise disposed of according to the directions of the person delivering them. The person delivering the goods is called the 'Bailor' and the person to whom they are delivered is called 'Bailee'.

Different Kinds of Bailment

The delivery of goods in bailment means for a temporary purpose. It may be either in the form of:

(*a*) Deposit: Goods kept for bailor's use.
(*b*) Hire: Goods delivered to the bailee for hire.
(*c*) Pawn: Goods delivered by way of security for money borrowed.

Liability of a Bailor

If the goods are bailed for hire, the bailor is responsible of any damage of the goods. Similarly in all cases of bailment, the bailee is bound to take care of the goods bailed to him. In either case, they are liable to pay an amount to compensate the damage or theft of the goods.

Definition of Pledge

The bailment of goods as security for payment of a debt or performance of a promise is called pledge. The bailor is in this case called the 'Pawnor'. The bailor is called the 'Pawnee'. Since a pledge or a pawn is a bailment of goods as a security for some debt, delivery of some movable or tangible property is necessary to complete the pledge. The pawnee is entitled to receive from the pawnor, extraordinary expenses incurred by him for the presentation of the goods pledged.

Agent

An agent is a person employed to do any act for another or to represent another in dealings with third person. The person for whom such act is done is called the principal.

Different Kinds of Agents

(1) Broker: He primarily establishes contact between the parties and gets brokerage. He does not possess goods in his name.
(2) Factor: He is entrusted with the possession of the goods and can sell to his name.
(3) Auctioneer: He is an agent for the seller and conducts auction sale on his behalf.
(4) Commission Agent: He merely buys or sells goods in the market on behalf of the seller against commission.
(5) Sub-Agent: He is a person employed and acting under the contract of the original agent.

Duties of an Agent

(*a*) An agent is bound to abide by the directions given by the principal.
(*b*) An agent is bound to conduct the business of the agency with reasonable diligence.
(*c*) An agent is bound to submit proper accounts to his principal on demand.
(*d*) It is the duty of an agent to communicate with his principal in case of difficulty and to obtain his instructions.
(*e*) He cannot delegate his authority to another unless authorized.

6.3.2 The sale of Goods Act 1872

The sale of movable goods comes under the purview of the act. It is a continuation of Contract Act. A contract of sale of goods is a contract whereby the seller transfers or agrees to transfer the goods to the buyer for a price. The contract of sales has two components:

(*a*) Sale
(*b*) Agreement to sell.

When the seller transfers the goods to the buyers against a price, there is sale but when the seller agrees to transfer the goods subject to some condition, which actually takes place at a future date, the seller undertakes an agreement to sell. When the condition is fulfilled, the agreement to sell becomes a sale by transfer of goods.

There is a difference between sale and hire purchase. In the case of a hire purchase agreement, the contract is nothing but bailment and the goods passes to the buyer only on completion of all the terms of the agreement. As such an agreement of hire purchase is not one for sale, but to pass ownership till all the installments are paid off.

Formalities of the Contract

A contract of sale may be made in any of the following ways:

(*a*) There may be immediate delivery of goods.
(*b*) The payment of price may be cleared earlier but the delivery of goods may take place at a later date.
(*c*) Delivery of goods and payment of the price may be done at the same time.

(*d*) It may also be agreed that the delivery or payment or both may be made in installments.

Subject Matter of the Contract

The subject matter of the contract of sale may be the goods which are existing or in possession of the seller or for the future goods which will be manufactured or produced or to be acquired by the seller after making the contract. Where the goods have perished before making of the contract and without seller's knowledge, the contract is void.

Conditions and Warranties

There may be certain stipulation in a contract of sale. They are of two types:

(*a*) Condition: A condition is a situation in the form of expressed statement or promise by a party or implied essential to the main purpose of the contract, the branch of which gives rise to a right to treat the contract as repudiated.

(*b*) Warranty: A warranty is a stipulation, the breach of which gives rise to a claim for damage but not a right to reject the goods.

In any case whether the stipulation is a condition or a warranty depends on the construction of the contract in each case.

Implied Conditions and Warranties

If there is no mention in the contract, the implied conditions and warranties in a sale of goods act are the following:

(*a*) Title of Goods: The seller has the right to sell the goods and that in case of an agreement to sell, he will have the right to sell the goods at the time when the property is to pass.

(*b*) Quiet Possession: The buyer shall have and enjoy quiet possession of the goods.

(*c*) Free from Charge: The goods shall be free from any charge in favour of any third party not declared or known to the buyer before or at the time when the contract is made.

(*d*) Quality or Fitness of Goods: The goods should be reasonably fit for the purpose for which they are required.

(*e*) Sale by Description: Where the goods are sold by description, the goods should really correspond with the description.

(*f*) Sale by Sample: When the contract is 'sale by sample' the bulk of the goods should be actually correspond with the sample in quality.

6.3.3 The Partnership Act 1932

The partnership act defines partnership as the relation between persons who have agreed to share profit of the business carried on by all or any of them acting for all.

Characteristics of Partnership

(*a*) *Contractual Relationship*: The partnership is formed only when a contract between a certain number of persons called partners take place. A minor cannot be a partner. A Hindu Joint Family firm does not fall in the category of partnership.

(*b*) *Plurality of Persons*: There must be at least two partners to form the partnership. However the numbers should not exceed twenty.

(*c*) *Existence of Business*: Since partnership implies business, where there is no business, there is no partnership.

(*d*) *Sharing of Profits*: The partnership agreement is made to carry on business with the object of making profit and sharing it among all the members.

(*e*) Mutual Agency: The business for which the partnership results must be carried on by all the partners or any one or more of them acting for all the partners.

(*f*) *Legal Implications*: A few important legal implications, which should be kept in mind while forming a partnership and conducting partnership business:

1. *Legal Position*: A partnership firm is only an association of individuals who collectively form a 'firm' which is only a word to describe the partners and it has no legal existence without the partners.
2. *Extent of Liability*: The liability of each partner for the debts of the firm is unlimited. The creditors enjoy the right to recover the financial debt from the private property of any or all partners.
3. *Nature of Partner's liability*: In a partnership firm the responsibility created is joint and rests on each of the partners. Any agreement to limit the liability of any partners may not be considered valid.
4. *Utmost Good Faith*: Each partner must be loyal and honest towards the other partners as the partnership form is founded on mutual confidence and trust.
5. *Implied Authority*: When a partner acts as management to perform regular acts on behalf and in the name of the firm, business transactions performed by him such as buying and selling of stock of the firm, the engagement and retrenchment of employees, the borrowing of money etc., is treated to be the act of the firm. The authority exercised by the partner can be treated as the partner's authority on behalf of other partners.
6. *Unanimity of the Consent*: Unanimous decision by all the partners of the firm is necessary for changing any policy matter including alteration of the partnership constitution. Majority decision does not apply in such cases.
7. *Non-transferability of Share or Interest*: As the name signifies, the partnership interest cannot be transferred to any other person. This may be done only when all other partners give their consent in favour of such transfer.
8. *Dissolution*: The partnership firm dissolves due to the death or insolvency of a partner if there is no agreement contrary to this. A partnership may be dissolved with the consent of all partners. It may also be dissolved, by the happening of an event, which makes the continuation of the partnership business unlawful. If the partnership is constituted for a limited term, it may be dissolved on expiry of the term. A court may dissolve a partnership under certain conditions.
9. *Settlement of Partnership Accounts*: When a partnership is dissolved, losses incurred by the firm are to be borne equally by the partners. Losses are to be divided in the same proposition as the profits, if the later were not equally divided. If the partners made unequal contribution towards a capital formation

of the firm but had enjoyed equal share of the profit, in that case, it is obligatory on the part of all the partners to contribute equally to raise the capital deficiency. The debts of the firm to outside partners are paid by selling the assets of the firm. The assets of the firm are also utilized for paying each partner for their advances made against capital contribution and paid in the same proportion as their advances.

10. *Partnership Deed*: Though it is not obligatory to have a partnership in writing but to avoid future troubles and disputes, there should be some written documents in the form of a deed. When the partnership is formed by a written agreement on stamped paper under the guidance of a lawyer, it is called the 'Article of Partnership' or 'Partnership Deed'. This Partnership deed defines the mutual relations among the partners. The partnership contract should contain the following information:
    (*a*) Name of firm together with the names of the partners.
    (*b*) Name of the business.
    (*c*) Duration of Partnership.
    (*d*) The amount of capital each partner contributes.
    (*e*) The sharing of profits and losses.
    (*f*) Division of work among partners for management of the firm.
    (*g*) Keeping accounts and audits.
    (*h*) How bank accounts are to be kept.
    (*i*) Authority for signing cheques and other documents.
    (*j*) Provisions to be made in event of death or retirement of any partner.
    (*k*) Provision for arbitration in case of disputes among the partners.
    (*l*) Arrangements for settlements in case of dissolution of partnership.

6.4 FORMS OF BUSINESS OWNERSHIP – A LEGAL ANALYSIS

6.4.1 The Proprietorship

A Proprietorship, is a business owned and controlled by one person and being the simplest form of a business enterprise it has several advantages such as:

1. Lack of restrictions,
2. Owner's enjoyment of all profits,
3. Owner's freedom to take all decisions,
4. Financial advantages,
5. Tax advantages, and
6. Secrecy.

1. Lack of restrictions

Lack of restrictions or minimum legal restriction is the distinguishing feature of a proprietorship concern. In a proprietorship the entrepreneur is required to file few reports and is not required to draw up legal document to commence his or her business nor is he or she required to pay any fees to set up his or her business. No formal registration is statutorily needed. Most common amongst the proprietorship are the sole proprietorship, i.e., one person operating the whole business.

2. Owner's enjoyment of all profits

One advantage of proprietorship is that the owner keeps to himself or herself all profit of his or her labor. Unlike other forms of ownership, in a proprietorship, there is no other person to share his or her profits, which in turn is a source of great personal satisfaction to him or her.

3. Owner's freedom to take all decisions

Another advantage of proprietorship is that the proprietor is free to make all decision. There is no other person who can weigh him down or create administrative problems for him or her. In this way he or she may freely concentrate on the business.

4. Financial advantages

One major advantage of a proprietorship is the financial advantage involved in this form of ownership. Personal reputation and personal assets stand behind the concern. Whenever needed the proprietor can draw upon both to augment his or her business resources.

5. Tax advantages

A proprietorship form of legal organisation has certain tax advantages which are not available to the other forms of business ownerships. Individual proprietorship income is taxed only once while corporate income is at occasions, taxed twice. Tax action with respect to all the forms of organisations is discussed separately.

6. Secrecy

Secrecy is another major advantage offered by proprietorship. In present day business atmosphere, the less a competitor know about one's business, the better off one is. In proprietorship the proprietor is required very few things to others, about his or her operations, he or she can keep business secrets to one self and the competitor and only guess estimates regarding its sales, profit margins and overall financial strength.

Disadvantages of Proprietorship

In spite of all the above mentioned advantage, there are some drawbacks associated with the proprietorship. In deciding whether the type of operation will suit him or her best for the business, the entrepreneur need to consider such things as:

1. Owner's probable lack of ability and experience

The owner may truly lack requisite ability and experience to run a business enterprise on one's own. Though this flaw in the entrepreneur's capability does not apply in sole proprietorship only, it could apply as well in partnership and companies. In the latter cases the lack of ability and experience may be compensated by the ability and experience of other partner/directors. In sole proprietorship since the decision-making is centralised in owner's hands flaw may become a debilitating one.

2. Difficulty in raising capital

The raising of capital single handed can be problem as the owner has only his or her own assets and goodwill to fell back upon, abetted by the assistance provided by the financial institutions. As a generalisation one person would have less to invest to meet the capital needs of a new small business than a group of owners. If the owner does not wise to share the ownership of the business, the alternatives for raising capital for the business are rather limited.

3. Limited life of the organisation

The life of the proprietorship depends solely on the proprietor. If he or she dies, becomes insolvent or permanently incapacitated or insane, the business may wind up. This has implications not only for the employees of the organisation but also for the creditors. It is this implication which finds an expression in the restrictions on credit granted to the sole proprietor. It is not uncommon to find credits requiring the proprietor to carry life insurance sufficient to meet the financial obligations of the proprietorship.

4. Limited size

There being only one owner of the business the account of capital that can be raised for operation and consequently the probability of attaining a large size are limited. This is especially true since the growth of the proprietorship is to a large degree dependent upon reinvested profits. As the capital that can be raised is limited the growth of the business can also attain only a limited size. The problem of size may also have managerial ramifications. Being the only owner the proprietor is responsible for carrying out all decision-making activities and quite a few of the operational one. This can become a burden as the business increases in size. Delegation of authority offers a solution, but the major decisions continue to be the owner's responsibility. It is then that he or she makes a conscious decision of whether or not to increase the size of the business enterprise any further.

5. Unlimited liability

By far as the greatest disadvantage of sole proprietorship is that of unlimited liability. The sole proprietor is personally responsible for all the debts that he or she incurs. The creditors having a claim on these debts can exercise it against both the business and the personal assets of the proprietor. For example if the proprietorship operation is worth Rupees 10 lakhs but the proprietor has debts of 25 lakhs, the creditors can sue the proprietor and force him or her to liquidate personal assets to pay the financial obligations. What this amounts to is that even though the proprietor believes that only part of his or her total capital is invested in the business, one is liable to the full extent of total personal assets for liabilities of the business. A damaging law suit lost, a serious accident involved injuries to employees, a critical marketing setback are some of the contingencies that can create liabilities for beyond investment and all other assets become liable investments and may be endangered.

Advantages Partnership

From the point of view of evaluating it as an organisational form, the flowing of partnership must be considered:

(a) Ease of organisation

As partnership is based on mutual contract between all the partners, it is relatively ease to form. The legal formalities associated with formation are minimal, so much so that registration of a partnership firm though desirable, is not obligatory.

(b) Combined talent, judgement and skill

The old maxim of two heads being better than one aptly applies to partnership. If there are three or four or more partners the chances that better decisions collectively will emerge are higher than in case of the proprietor operating alone. Pooling of skills, especially when each partner specialises in a different area gives the firm a competitive advantage of collective expertise.

(c) Increased sources of capital and credit

We have just seen that the sole proprietorship suffers from the limitation of limited capital because there is only one individual to invest his or her assets and being in credit. A partnership can overcome this problem to certain extent by bringing into association more people with capital to invest as well as personal assets that can be used as collateral for bank loans and other credit. The lending institutions also perceive less risk in granting credit to a partnership than to a proprietorship because the risk of loss is spread over a number of people rather than only one.

(d) Improved chances of growth

Consequent upon the increased sources of capital and credit and better decision-making potential, the partnership is in a much better position to expand and grow than proprietorship. Being managed by a group of people, a partnership has both monetary and managerial resources to manage larger facilities and more employees. Therefore, as the operations expand in size, the owners are able to maintain effective control.

(e) Tax advantage

From the taxation point of view partnership seems to be the most desirable form of the organisation as the taxation rates applicable are lower than both the other forms in question.

Disadvantages of Partnership

In spite of it's numerous advantages the partnership also has some important disadvantages which must be seriously consider before opting for this form of organisation:

1. Unlimited liability

As already noted, unlimited liability is an important characteristic of partnership. Just as this condition is applicable to proprietorship, it becomes an even more serious limitation in partnership. Not only is a partner liable to the extent of one's personal assets, for the debts of the firm, but he is also responsible to the full extent of one's resources for the debts contraded by other partner. Similarly, as profits and losses are to be shared between the partners even if one partner cannot come up with his or her share of the losses, the others will have to make up deficits.

2. Limited life

If any partner dies, becomes insane or is otherwise incapacitated or simply wants to withdraw from the business, the partnership gets terminated. As the number of partners increases, the probability of occurrence of these contingencies goes higher. This creates problems of continuity in business.

3. Divided authority

We just talked about the maxim of two heads being better than one, carried to an extreme the situation may turn into "too many cooks spoil the broth". As long as each partner restricts his or her activities to one's defined area of operation, the problem of divided authority can be checked. However, other areas like policy formulation for the whole firm, financing plans, evolving personnel policy and ideas on expansion can create possibilities for conflicting authority.

4. Danger of personal disagreements

Being an association of people a partnership is always open to the danger of disagreement between its members which at times may become extremely serious. Even if a partnership agreement is thoroughly detailed, clauses may be subject to different interpretations. Some partners may wilfully exceed their defined authority and discontent may develop because of diverse working style and conflicting egos. Many successful partnership firms have been dissolved of serious disagreement between the partners.

Advantage of a Company

The important among the advantage of a company are:

(*a*) **Limited liability:** The advantage of limited liability offered by a company forms an effective incentive for choosing this form of organisation as the shareholders are fully aware that they stand to lose no more than that they have agreed to invest in the business.

(*b*) **Perpetual existence:** Continuity to the business is ensured as unlike a partnership or a proprietorship, a company enjoys perpetual succession. Death, incapacity or insanity of the shareholder do not affect the corporate existence of the company as the shares simply get transferred to the legal heirs who can sell them further if they do not want to retain the share contingencies like insolvency of the shareholder or selling of the share by him or her also do not bring the life of the company to an end. As these factors would only result in the change of ownership of shares.

(*c*) **Transferability of shares:** Ease of transferor of interest of a company represents another major advantage of companies. The very fact that you can transfer your interest anytime you want to, facilitates both investment and disinvestments decision in this form of organisation.

(*d*) **Expansion potential:** In comparison to proprietorship and partnership, the company has far greater potential for raising capital through issue of shares. This has implications for both ease and value for expansion.

(*e*) **Representative management:** Both proprietorship and partnership are characterized by direct management in that the owner/partner directly participate in the management of the organisation. A company on the other hand is characterized by representative management in that shareholders elect the directors to manage the company. The directors in turn manage the company as agents and trustees of the company, for the benefit of the company. If found to be deficient in performing their duties, any director may be removed. In addition to the Board of directors, the company also relies on bringing in specialists as managers to manage the affair of the company, which augurs well for efficiency and management.

Disadvantages of a Company

(*a*) **Lack of secrecy:** As the company has to make various statements available to the registrar of Companies and Financial Institutions, there is much less confidentiality of operations as compared to the other forms of organisation. In addition, the company has to provide an annual report to every shareholder, which further reduces the degree of secrecy, as everyone including the competitors can find out details of all financial data.

(*b*) **Legalities of formation:** Being a creation of law, a company involves far more legal formalities of formation in comparison to the other two forms. These includes registration and pre-registration formalities like preparation of documents entering into pre-incorporation contracts, obtaining the consent of directors and furnishing the stamp duty. All these steps considerably lessen the ease of formation characterising the other forms of organisation.

(*c*) **Legal restriction:** The operations of a company are far more regulated by the comprehensive legislation of the companies act. Almost all aspects of its management and operation must comply with the provisions of the Act. In addition to the company Act, several other Acts impose restrictions on the activities of companies in India.

(*d*) **Heavy taxation:** Companies are subject to heavier taxation rates. There is also an incidence of double taxation in that after deducting tax, when the company pays dividend to its shareholders, the individual shareholder is also liable to pay personal income tax on all dividends recovered depending upon their respective tax brackets.

7

Information Technology

7.1 INFORMATION TECHNOLOGY NEEDS FOR ENTREPRENEURS

Today, every business needs Information Technology. Entrepreneurs may have to rely on technology to handle most routine business operations, from maintaining financial records, to processing orders, to staying in contact with suppliers and customers. Because technology is so central to running a business today, one needs to plan what kinds of technology will be used and how to use it.

7.1.1 Why An Information Technology Plan is Needed?

Many decisions you make about your technology, may be costly or cumbersome to change later. When outlining your technology plan, keep in mind how your organisation might grow or change. Try to choose technology that is flexible enough to grow and change with time and need. As much as possible, choose technology that, while meeting your needs, is simpler rather than overly complex. All those extra "features" may just make your technology (whether it be a software program or a telephone) harder to use.

7.1.2 Uses of Information Technology

When you examine your business operations, look at which functions require or could benefit from Information Technology. Following are the common business processes that may need information technology:

1. Finance, accounting & taxes
2. Order receiving and tracking
3. Order fulfillment/shipping
4. Inventory management
5. Database management: customer, product, supplier, inventory, etc.
6. Mailing lists
7. Communication with customers
8. Internal communication
9. Presentations

10. Desktop publishing/graphics
11. Personnel/human resources management
12. Production: design, cost-tracking, supply chain management, etc.
13. Internet marketing/Web site/E-mail
14. Sales Analysis

7.1.3 Issues in Choosing Information Technology

Key issues when choosing information technology include:

1. Functions
2. Ease of use
3. Cost
4. Security
5. Ability to be upgraded and/or expanded
6. Integration with existing data, technology, systems, etc.

7.2 INFORMATION TECHNOLOGY TOOLS

7.2.1 The Fax

Faxes can often be the fastest and most efficient means of transferring a document. It is the most popular among businesses. More importantly, people are used to it being around and have been relying on fax far longer than any other data transfer tool. Simplicity and low cost price is the key to fax. Set up is minimal and provided you have a telephone line and connection you can plug the machine in and the rest will come naturally. As long as you have paper in the feeder you will be able to send and receive single or multiple documents in a short time frame, with a minimum amount of fuss and without paying high price.

Fax vs E-mail: With email being cheaper and readily available, why you invest in a fax machine at all? If you and your clients are more reliant on e-mail this is perhaps the way to stay. But what if it goes wrong and that an important document needs to be sent immediately? This is one scenario where a fax machine can be a crucial tool. Fax and e-mail complement each other exceptionally well, particularly if one goes wrong. However, the vast majority of people still rely on fax as a core means of communication.

Fax has a number of major advantages over e-mail, particularly for small businesses. Small businesses prefer to use fax when sending sensitive documents, customer quotes and prospects as well as copies of invoices and diagrams. Small firms are unsure about the safety and relevance of e-mail. This shows that the comfort factor of fax is ever present and that its speed, efficiency and low cost factor is more suited to smaller organisation.

Fax is more reliable as you know that it's been sent and waiting for the recipient while with an e-mail you may not be sure about the delivery.

There are two main variations of fax machine on the market today – "Thermal Roll" and "Plain Paper". Within the plain paper category are Inkjet and Laser versions. More up-to-date fax alternatives include faxing from a PC and the Internet. Your choice will depend on what business you are in, the volume of faxes you are sending or receiving and how much you are willing to spend.

7.2.2 Personal Computers & E-mail Connection

It's no longer worth speculating, if you're starting almost any type of business you need a computer and e-mail connection. You might get away without one but you won't be as organized, efficient or professional as you could be, and as you won't be online, you'll be missing out on engaging any number of contacts and potential customers.

To help demonstrate what using a personal computer & e-mail can add to your business, here's a list of some of the main advantages:

E-mail Communication: E-mail is an easy, fast and least expensive form of communication. Being in touch and continuous communication is very easy through e-mail for any business.

Online Communication: Virtually every type of business communication is now online. You can pay bills, order stock, file tax returns, network, advertise for staff and, of course, sell your products. What's more you can do all of this when it is convenient for you instead of squeezing in trips to the bank.

Presentation: Every business has to produce literature of some kind or another, whether it be promotional brochures; letters; invoices; posters or staff docodocuments. Producing your own is simple. It saves printing costs and gives an air of efficiency. You can also make a Video Compact Disc (VCD) of your Company Profile Presentation and send it to your potential customers.

Organisation: If you're organised, chances are that you're efficient. Your accounts, stock level and orders, sales and contact details should be stored on computer so that if you need to know anything about your business, it's only a click away.

Data control: Data has never been so important or valuable. If you collect the details of your customers you can contact them again when you're running a special offer or to let them know about new lines you're releasing. By having the details of a solid customer base stored on computer, you can do much of your marketing yourself.

Security: 'The paperless office' might be a myth, but it's important to ensure all your organisation documentation and records are stored on file. Not only does it save space, but back-up copies can be invaluable in the unfortunate case of fire, flooding or theft.

Efficiency: Incorporating a computer into your business, in the simple terms, should make you more efficient. It should save you time and money that you can reinvest into actually running and growing your business.

7.2.3 Printer

The printer is now an essential business tool. Used wisely it'll create professional documents and promotional literature, saving you money and time.

It's possible to print your own business cards, letter-headed paper, promotional brochures, posters, labels, special offer displays, flyers, invoices, supplier contracts, employee contracts and much more.

In the average small business their is always the need to print standard word documents, e-mails or reports. If these are substantial in length or number, you'll need a printer that can cope with the output and that is efficient.

7.2.4 Photocopier

Today, organisations cannot operate effectively without one. The good news is that modern small-office copiers are probably cheaper and better featured than you expect.

Size and Colour: Copiers in large offices often support A3 as well as ordinary A4 paper. In the small business startup, you would probably only consider an A3-capable device for task-specific reasons. The fast majority of buyers will only be interested in A4, which is good for the widest variety of documents from business correspondence to archival copies. Many black-and-white conventional photocopiers have been designed especially for small office use, intended to sit on a desktop rather than on a floor-standing cabinet, and are priced accordingly.

Speed and Volume: Photocopiers are usually quoted as outputting a certain number of 'pages per minute' (ppm) for short. Cheap desktop copiers typically rate at 4 ppm, rising through 6 ppm, 8 ppm and 12 ppm before the price rises above what an average small business would want to pay. High-end copiers are available which run out as many as 100 ppm, but then you're talking about a five-figure investment or a major lease arrangement.

If you do not have the funds to buy one, you can also opt to hire one on terms such as "pay per page" basis while all the maintenance is the supplier's responsibility.

7.2.5 Scanner

While in the past, the scanner was seen as a specialist product, it has now become a staple in many offices. Prices are coming down all the time and this has undoubtedly helped with their popularity. But in addition to being increasingly affordable, the growth of the Internet and the need to create electronic images for web pages is also driving the trend. For many businesses it has long been a crucial piece of equipment. These include estate agents, photographers, publishing houses etc.

From adding a bit more spice to your business with colourful posters and a snazzy company logo to scanning in your own photographs or slides to create a newsletter, a scanner is very helpful.

There are two main forms of scanner that you may wish to consider: Flatbed and Film scanners.

Flatbed scanners: They are more commonly used and are so named because of their flat surfaces and work in very much the same way as printers except that the end product ends up on your PC rather than on an in-tray.

Film scanners: The other principal form is film scanners. These are more associated with the scanning of photographs, slides and negatives and are often more expensive than their flatbed counterparts.

7.2.6 Digital Camera

When you need to send a picture of the product you are offering to one of your customers, you can immediately take a picture using a digital camera and send the digital picture via e-mail. In this way you can save a lot of time and be highly effective. Customer can see the product and can make a purchase decision. A number of Digital cameras are available and the quality of picture depends on the "megapixels" they offer. Currently the good ones are between 3 to 5.5 Megapixels.

7.2.7 Mobile Phone

Mobile phone has become "a must" in any form of business communication. Apart from the simple phone conversation, Short Messaging Service (SMS) has become a highly effective marketing tool. Following things can be done using SMS in a small business:

- Offering Goods & Services to customers
- Promoting Goods & Services
- Confirming Price
- Confirming Orders
- SMS banking
- Buying and selling goods & services
- Information hunting

Latest mobile phones come with following features:

- Personal Digital Assistant & Organizer
- Small PC with Word Processing & Spreadsheet software
- Still & Video Camera
- E-mail & Internet facility
- Wireless connectivity

7.3 MANAGEMENT INFORMATION SYSTEM (MIS)

Management information relates to the top management tasks of deciding on objectives of the organisation on the levels and the kinds of resources required to attain the objectives and on the policies that govern the acquisition, use and disposition of resources.

Management & information can be categorized into three areas: (1) Strategic Planning Information (2) Management Control Information (3) Operational Information.

Strategic planning depends heavily on information external to a specific organisation. When combined with internal data, management can estimate expected results. Management Control Information tells about goal congruence. It helps managers to take those actions which are in the best interests of the Organisation. It enables managers to see that resources are being used efficiently and effectively in meeting the organisational goals. Three types of information are needed for management control: (*a*) Cost by responsibility centers, direct programme cost and full programme costs including indirect costs. Management Control Information ties together various sub-activities in a coherent way so that managers can gauge resources utilization and compare expected with actual results. Management Control Information is often interdepartmental.

Operational information pertains to those day to day activities of the organisation and helps assure that specific tasks are performed effectively and efficiently. It also includes the production of routine and necessary information. Such as financial accounting, payrolls, personnel rosters, equipment inventories and logistics. Operational Information such as, scheduling work flow through a department or producing payroll, generally originates in one department.

Systems for handling each of these categories differ as a result of the varying degree to which the tasks can be well defined, operational information can be well defined and easily reduced to a routine of a series of instructions whereas strategic information is difficult to define. Control information falls in between.

Computerised Information systems – The technical advancements in computer hardware have forced improvement in software. This rapid progress has made possible economical and comprehensive information systems that are certain to have a strong impact on all functions of management in the future, whereas in the past, side rules were essential for engineers and calculators were important to accountants, the modern computers now serve as the powerful foundation for management information system. At first computers were of particular value for large organisations. In future as a result of the growing availability of data processing centers which sell computer service to small users and the development of small inexpensive computers, management of firms of all sizes find the same computerised systems within their capabilities. The only obstacle to universal use of computer information systems is the lack of awareness on the part of human being of the tremendous power now available to them. Managers need not understand the technical matters of computers to gain this power any more than an automobile driver needs to be a mechanic or a child in turning on a light or starting a toy needs to understand electricity.

8

An Overview

8.1 MANAGING A SMALL ENTERPRISE WITH A PERFORMANCE ASSESSMENT DESIGN

Managing a business enterprise is to balance a variety of needs and goals. This requires a search for right objectives, which are needed in every area where performance and results directly and vitally affect the survival and prosperity of the enterprise.

If profit, for instance, is considered as prime concern, sometimes this may endanger the survival of the enterprise because profit making may undermine the future. The products most easily saleable may undermine those products that have the market for tomorrow. Therefore rational discussions to achieve future goals are to be made on sound foundation of facts and reliable measurements of the effects and validity of actions and decisions. Whatever the business, whatever the economic conditions, whatever the size of business, there are some key areas, where objective of performance and results are to be set. The vital areas are: Market standing, innovation, productivity, physical and financial resources, profitability, managerial performance, worker's attitude and public responsibility. The real difficulty lies not in determining objectives but in deciding how to set them. What should be measured in each area and what yardstick of measurement should be applied. It should be remembered that whatever should be measured, they need to be relevant, visible, tangible and achievable.

PERFORMANCE ASSESSMENT DESIGN*

Key Areas Measurement	Objectives
	Determining Factors to be Measured
Market Standing (Buyer's behavior, competitors behavior, market potential)	1. Existing products in the present market in terms of money value.

(Contd.)

Key Areas Measurement	Objectives
	2. Existing products in the new market in terms of money value. 3. Existing products that should be abandoned. 4. New products needed in existing market in terms of market share and money value. 5. New markets and new products development in terms of money value and market share. 6. Distribution: Cost and pricing policy.
Innovation (Technological Changes)	1. Product Improvement to satisfy marketing goal. 2. New product/services to attain marketing goals that may make present products obsolete.
Productivity (Resources used, utilized those and the yield)	1. Measurement of contributed value: All the efforts of the enterprise and the entire reward received for efforts. Ratio of contributed value to total revenue
Physical and Financial Resources (Planning for adequate supply of physical and financial resources needed to attain the goals set for market standing and innovation)	1. Capital Budget: how much capital is required and in what form and from where it will come. It is mainly the job of financial specialists.
Productivity (Minimum of Profit needed for survival and prosperity of the enterprise)	1. Minimum Concept: Profit measures not the maximum but the minimum cost of staying in the business. 2. Tools for measuring profit, Break-even point analysis, Profit as percentage of sale, return on investment and other financial ratio analysis.
Managerial Performance **Worker's Attitude** **Public Responsibility**	These key areas mainly deals with human factors. We can not simply add them together or subtract them from one another. Qualitative standards rather than quantitative measurements are needed.

* Adapted from Practice of Management-Peter Drucker.

Managerial performance depends on the spirit of organization, structure of management and development of future managers who believe in **'Personal Touch'** and **'Quick Response'.**

Workers attitude mainly depend on union reactions. Attempts are always to be made to buildup a paternal relationship as in Japan.

Objectives in the field of public responsibility have to be setup according to the social and political conditions and on the basis of beliefs of management and its financial strength.

Each and every enterprise requires its own balance at different times differently. It is achieved by budgeting. Decisions require judgment and it will be sound only when it is based on sound analysis. Objections set in the key areas are vital to pilot any business enterprise.

8.2 DEMANDS FROM FUTURE BUSINESS MANAGERS AND NEW GENERE OF ENTREPRENEURS

The managers, the life giving and dynamic elements in the 'Management Administration' of any business enterprise determine its success and survival. With the complexity of changing technologies and business relationship, modern business enterprise demand that a manager become an elite of brains and education. Entrance to this class is based more and more on management degrees. The career managerial class is gradually obtaining increasing amount of power and threatens to become an autonomous class. The notion may be an overstatement but there is no doubt that educated, trained and experienced managers are becoming powerful and lead in the world of business today. It is deeply perceived that there is a need for the development of better thinking by a manager and his perspective should be based on a literally educated outlook of life because a liberal point of view emphasizes on freedom to choose from the widest range of possibilities by discovering new horizon. A liberally oriented manager expands his perspectives with utmost freedom to choose the best course of action.

The process of management is also undergoing rapid changes. A business manager must understand his role under changing conditions, which relates to

1. Complex consumer behaviour
2. Factors of production
3. Environment
4. Globalisation

What is needed, in the face of changing conditions, is the development of a future business manager equal to the tasks of tomorrow. The future business manager must be dynamic and must aim at challenging all-round growth and self-development. The process must focus on gainful performance rather than promises and on tomorrow's requirement rather than on those of today.

Peter Drucker has summerised the new demands from a business manager of tomorrow into seven new tasks:

1. He must manage by objectives
2. He must take more risks and for a longer period ahead. And risk taking will have to be made at lower levels. The manager must therefore be able to calculate each risk to choose the most advantageous risk alternatives, to establish in advance what he expects to happen and to control his subsequent course of action as events bear out or deny his expectations.
3. He must be able to make strategic decisions.
4. He must be able to build an integrated team, each member of which is capable to managing and of measuring his own performance and results in relation to the common objectives.
5. He must be able to communicate information fast and clearly. He will be able to motivate people. He must in other words be able to obtain the responsible participation of other managers, of the professional specialists and all workers.

6. The business manager of tomorrow must be able to see the business as a whole and to integrate his function with it.
7. The business manager of tomorrow will have to be able to relate his product and industry to the total environment, to find what is significant in it and take it in to account in his decisions and actions. And increasingly the field of vision of tomorrow's business manager will have to take in developments outside his own market and his own country. Increasingly he will have to learn to see economic, political and social development on worldwide scale and to integrate worldwide trends into his own decision to face global market.

To accept the challenges of tomorrow's management task, business manager of the day need advanced management education. Intellectual and conceptual education will not alone enable the business manager of today to accomplish the task of tomorrow. It will demand vision, courage, responsibility and above all integrity.

8.3 CHANGES IN MANAGEMENT CONCEPTS*

Models for Dealing with Changes

There was a time when the field of management was engaged primarily to the managers of Industrial plants. Recently managers in public sector, educational institutions, consulting firms, etc. have found that they have many common problems. So, the application of management concepts and techniques to varied types of organisations spreads and will continue to spread. Changes in the environment changes in consumer behaviour, changes in factors of productions and changes in society including increase in the size of consumer markets and the segmentation of markets into strata are obvious changes. Values, expectations and aspirations are continually being transformed.

As a result of changes, the manager faces a dilemma. The new managerial perceptions are central to the area of ecology the study of man and his environment. There may be three models developed to deal with the resistance and other aspects of human behaviour – (*a*) planned change model with behaviour, (*b*) decision-making model and (*c*) systems model.

(*a*) a fairly recent development in managerial training – Sensitivity Training which deals with human learning and behavioural change and usually occurs in group. The trainer is from outside and feed back the persons are encouraged to understand the impact they make upon others and are given support if they want to make any behavioural adaptations. In many instances the change require changes in attitudes through a threefold process. In a training group, called T-group conditions exist for individual behaviour change by first focusing upon 'here and now' situations. In other words, the group creates experiences which are shared by all members, thus forming a common bond. The experiences are reality type and personal. The trainer adds a second ingradient to the 'here and now' experiences, the idea of feed back. Each participant is encouraged to respond to the experiences, stating how he views

* Adapted from *Dynamics of Management* by J. Doglas, University of Kentucky.

them and there impact on him. Eventually the reality as perceived by the other group members becomes the behavioural bench-mark for the participant desiring change. The third condition for human learning in the group situations is unfreezing. Unfreezing means that a period of unlearning or shaking up usually take place before change can occur. The purpose of this short introduction to sensitivity training is to make aware of this potentially powerful tool for human change.

(*b*) **Changes in decision-making:** The decision world of the manager calls for adjustment, adaptation and comparison of alternatives emerging from the specific environment rather than decisions structured from static goals and objectives. The reality is change and the management posture in response.

Systems Change: The application of systems and process to manager's job marks a significant change in the field of management. His job is defined in terms of the input, through put, output and feedback of the system he operates. One constant demand upon him is to monitor the system, to keep the system at a state of dynamic equilibrium and to make continuity type decisions. The manager must know when and where to change the behaviour or to encourage change in others. The orientation is toward operating in the world as it really is rather than in a prescribed, artificial world. Change is inter dependence of all related parts and a better insight into the nature of systems. Development in systems theory and their application to organisations have caused managers to have renewed interest about them. Inflation, unemployment and poverty have significant impact on all organisations. The new management perceptions are central to the area of ecology the study of man and his environment. Even though the rise of environment was done by man's misuse of technology, the technology itself cannot be destroyed. If man applies his technological skill to the environmental problems, there may by an exhaustless automobiles, a noiseless aeroplane, new method of reducing and coping with wastes – radioactive sewage gas and liquid and new modes of transportation. Managers live in a changing world – a world in need of responsible innovation as well as responsible response.

8.4 MOTIVATION FOR HIGH STANDARDS OF PERFORMANCE* – SEARCH FOR A NEW HORIZON

Any enterprise needs people of high standards of performance to achieve the goal. A question arises what motivation is needed. The answer may be employee satisfaction. But this is meaningless even if it means something, employee satisfaction may not be sufficient motivation to fulfill the needs of the enterprise.

An employee may be satisfied with his job because he really finds fulfillment in it. We may also be satisfied because job permits him somehow to passion. An employee may be dissatisfied because he is genuinely discontented. He also may be dissatisfied because he wants to do a better job, wants to improve his own work and also of his group. This dissatisfaction is the most valuable attitude any enterprise may have among the employees and the most real expression of pride in job and work and of responsibility. As a matter

* Adapted from Human Organisation for Peak Performance by P.F. Drucker.

of fact dissatisfaction that is discontent from dissatisfaction that is the desire to do a better job is most valuable.

There is no standards to measure what degree of satisfaction is satisfactory. Nobody knows which of the thing that we are trying to measure interms of satisfaction have any effect or impact on behaviour and performance or how much impact they have. Is satisfaction with co-employee more important in motivating people to work than satisfaction with physical working conditions? Which of them is important? There is no clear direction. But satisfaction is above all inadequate as motivation. It is passive acquiescence. An employee who is deeply dissatisfied may quit or may become bitter. But what does an employee do, who is satisfied? After all the enterprise must demand of the employee that he must do something willingly and with personal involvement. Then it becomes performance and not just acquiessence. It becomes responsibility not satisfaction, is the only thing that will serve.

Responsibility cannot be bought for money. Financial rewards and incentives are important but they work largely negatively. Discontent with financial rewards is a powerful disincentive, undermining and corroding responsibility for performance. But satisfaction with monitory rewards is not a sufficient positive motivation. It motivates only where other things have made the employee ready to assure responsibility. Experience shows that incentive pay for increased work. The incentive pay produces better output where there is already a willingness to perform better otherwise it is inflectual a sabotage.

It does not matter whether the worker wants responsibility or not. The enterprise must demand it of him. The enterprise needs performance.

There are four ways by which we can attempt to reach the goal of the responsible employee. There are (*a*) careful placement, (*b*) high standards of performance (*c*) providing the employee with the information needed to control himself (*d*) opportunities for participation that will give him a managerial vision.

A systematic, serious and continual effort to place people right has already been proved a pre-requisite to high motivation. Nothing challenges men as effectively to improve performance as a job that makes high demands on them. Nothing gives them more pride of accomplishment. To focus on the best that can just be reached by constant effort and ability always build motivation. This does not mean that one should drive people. On the contrary one must let them drive themselves. But the only way to do this is to focus their vision on a high goal.

Output standard for the average employee are always minimum standards because he considers the standard as normal. But a good employee who can easily bit the standard is likely to be affected adversely. He feels that he is keeping his output low for the interest of the less competent fellow-employee inspite of his our capability to reach higher standard. This is one way of rotting ones ownself. The IBM decision to abolish general standard and let the individual employee workout his own norm was sound. This is instead of starting out with what an employee can do physically an enterprise may start with what an employee needs to contribute. The enterprise must spell out for each job what it has to contribute to the attainment of the objectives of the organisation or its survival. To motivate the employees to peak performance, it is equally important that management set and enforce on itself high standards for its own performance of those functions that determine the employees ability to perform.

Every organisation requires information to measure work against the set objectives. The rules for procedures and information that apply to managers, apply to workers as well. The employee should be enabled to control, measure and guide his own performance. He should know how he is doing without being told. The employee must also take the responsibility for the consequences of his actions. He should know his work relates to the work of the whole. He should know what he contributes to the enterprise.

Placement, performance standards and information are conditions for the motivation of responsibility. The employee will assume responsibility for peak performance only if he has a managerial vision, that is, if he looks to the enterprise as if he were a manager responsible through his performance for its success and survival. The vision he can only attain through the experience of participation. People are proud if they have done something to be proud of. People have a sense of accomplishment only if they have accomplished something. They feel important if their work is important.

8.5 DECISIONS IN INTERNATIONAL MARKETING*

The Complexity of the international marketing environment – the variation within and between nations of economic, political, legal, cultural and business factors requires the international marketer to proceed extremely carefully in deciding whether to market abroad, An enterprise faces five types of decisions – (1) The international marketing decisions determines whether the foreign opportunities and the organisation's resources are attractive enough to justify a general interest in marketing abroad (2) The market selection decision determines which foreign markets to enter. (3) The entry and operating decision determines the best way to enter and operate in an attractive foreign market (4) The marketing mix decision develops an appropriate product, price, distribution, and promotional programme for that market (5) The marketing organisation decision determines the best way for the organisation to achieve and maintain control over its international business operation.

Any enterprise gets involved in international marketing in two ways: (*a*) approached by some one, may be a domestic exporter or a foreign importer. An enterprise may find suddenly itself confronted with an opportunity to sell abroad or any organisation may start to think. On its own about marketing abroad due to our capacity or for better opportunity. Thus an organisation can be pushed or pulled in international marketing only when both opportunity and organisational resources are sound. Yet the real danger lies in estimating market potential of any selected market. Published market data hardly exists. Trade associations may not make their data available. Necessary data from marketing research agencies may not be available also. Foreign buyers may not also be found very much cooperative. Forecasting the future market potential is also difficult to make. Besides these difficulties, there are other hurdles like forecasting of costs and margin and estimating the rate of return on investment. Under the circumstances, organisations interested in international market, have there major options before them – (1) exporting, (2) Joint venture and (2) direct investment abroad. Any organisation may use different entry and operating strategies in different market.

---

* Adapted from Marketing Management by Philip Kotler.

Alternative entry and operating strategies in a foreign market.

I Export	II Joint Venture	III Direct Investment	IV Multinational Marketing
(*a*) Direct Export	(*a*) Licensing	(*a*) Assembly	
(*b*) Indirect Export	(*b*) Contract Manufacturing	(*b*) Manufacturing	
	(*c*) Management contracting		
	(*d*) Joint Ownership Venture		

I **Direct Export** – Exporter who are approached by foreign buyers will like to undertake direct export instead of middlemen. The process continues till the market has grown to sufficient size to justify undertaking their own activity. The investment and risk are greater but so is the potential return.

II **Joint Venture** – It means to set up production and marketing in association with organisations in the foreign country. Joint venture differs from direct investment. Four types of Joint venture can be formed (1) Licensing – the licenser enters into an agreement with a licenser in the foreign market, offering him the right to use a manufacturing process, trademark patent, trade secret or some other thing of value for a fee or royalty. Licensing has potential disadvantages in that the licenser has less control over the licensee. Further more if the licensee is very successful, he may find that he has set up a competitor. To avoid this danger, the licenser must establish a mutual advantage in working together and a key to doing this is to remain in innovative so that the license continues to depend on him (2) Contract manufacturing – It is an option to contract with local manufacturers to produce the product, contract manufacturing has the drawback of less control over the manufacturing process and the less of potential profits on manufacturing. On the other hand, it offers the manufacturers a chance to get started faster with less risk and with the opportunity to possibly form a partnership or lay out the local manufacturer if his facility operates efficiently.

3. **Management Contracting** – In this case the domestic company agree to supply the management Know-how to a Foreign Company that is willing to supply the capital. The domestic company is really exporting management service rather than its own products. Management contracting is a low risk method of getting into foreign market and it starts yielding income right from the beginning.
4. **Joint Ownership Venture** – An increasingly popular arrangement is for foreign investors to join with local investors to create a local business in which they share a joint ownership and control. The two parties form a new business venture. Joint ownership have certain drawbacks for the foreign firm. The partner may disagree over investment marketing or other policies. Further more, joint venturing can hamper the plans of a multinational company seeking to carry out specific manufacturing and marketing policies on a world wide basis. The agreement may also make it hard for the foreign firm to enter other markets where its partner

already operates. Inspite of all there potential disadvantages, joint ownership is often most attractive of several alternatives.

III **Direct Investment** – The ultimate form of involvement in a foreign market is unilateral investment in a foreign based manufacturing facilities. The advantages of direct investment are many (*a*) the company may secure real cost economics in the form of cheaper labour or raw materials, incentives of any form freight savings, etc. (*b*) the company will gain a better image in the host country because it demonstrates its concern with that country's future. (*c*) the company develops a deeper relationship with Govt., customers, local suppliers and distributors enabling it to make a better adaptation of its products to the local marketing environment. (*d*) the company retains full control over the investment and therefore can develop manufacturing and marketing polices that serves its long-term international objectives.

The main disadvantage is that the company has exposed a large investment to certain risks, sueles, devalued currpucies, worsening markets or expropriation.

Manufacturing: The company has to decide whether to create a complete manufacturing facility or only assembly facility. The former which requires considerably more investment is justified if there are considerable cost savings in conducting the whole manufacturing process abroad.

Assembly: Sometimes a company find it advantageous to permit its investment to an assembly operations for cost savings and tax exemptions or taxes at lower rates. Another possible source of savings occur when some components can be secured cheaper from local suppliers. For these or other reasons, assembly plans have often been resorted to.

IV **Multinational Marketing:** A global marketer who operates in many countries including 'home-market' is called Multinational Corporation. The Multinational corporation is defined as a company which has a direct investment base in several countries. The top management and staff are involved in the worldwide planning of manufacturing facilities, marketing policies, financial flows, and logistical systems. The various operating units around the world report directly to the chief executive, not to head of an international division. The Company trains its, executives in world wide operations, not just domestic or international. Management talents, are recruited from many countries, components and supplies are purchased where they can be obtained at the least cost and investment are made where the anticipated returns are greatest.

8.6 SOCIAL RESPONSIBILITY OF BUSINESS & INDUSTRY

Social responsibility is the personal obligation of everyone as he acts in his own interest, to assure that the rights and legitimate interest of all others are not fringed as defined by Koontz & O'Donnell eminent management authorities.

The concept of local responsibility is not unknown to Indian Business & Industrial Houses. Profit may be the prime consideration in business but various Industrial houses carryout a wide range of social activities in the field of public health, employee welfare,

Housing, education, environmental protection, resource conservation etc. The whole internal responsibilities of Business Houses can be divided into four main areas:

1. Responsibility towards employees
2. Responsibility towards govt.
3. Responsibility towards owners
4. Responsibility towards consumer apart from social responsibilities.

If Business Houses fail to shoulder the social responsibilities, society may bring them under legal framework. This is why business ethics are of much importance to business. The term business ethics indicates some moral obligations, which the society demands from Business Houses. Business ethics are derived from social values. They lay down the norms of behavior for the business actions.

The council for Fair Business practice established in 1966 have laid down some ethical principles applicable to business. These are:

(*a*) Charge only fair and reasonable price and take every possible step to ensure that the prices to be charged to the consumer are brought to notice.
(*b*) To take every possible step to ensure that the dealers do not charge prices higher than fixed.
(*c*) In times of scarcity, not to withheld or suppress stocks of goods with a view to hoarding profiteering.
(*d*) Not to produce or trade inspurious goods standards lower than specified.
(*e*) Not to adulterate goods supplied.
(*f*) Not to publish misleading advertisement.
(*g*) To invoice goods exported or imported at their correct prices.
(*h*) To maintain accuracy in weight and measures of goods offered for sale.
(*i*) Not to deal knowingly in smuggled goods.
(*j*) Providing after-sales-service where necessary and possible.
(*k*) Honoring the fundamental right of the consumers like, Right of safety, Right of choose, Right to information and Right to be heard.
(*l*) Discharging social responsibilities and the responsibility to protect the environment and nature's infrastructure.
(*m*) Ensuring that the product warranty is offered in simple, unambiguous and concise language, highlights the rights of consumers under it.

An entrepreneur has to do business keeping in view the welfare of the society and also certain ethics. The development of business and industry has gone a very favorable and significant changes towards society. The business community itself has realized its obligations to society. The social responsibilities have increased due to some reasons such as,

(*a*) Changed public expectations of business
(*b*) Society creating better environment for business
(*c*) Government rules and regulations etc. Social responsibility is an obligation of Business Houses to take actions, which protect and improve the welfare of society as a whole along with their own interest.

9

Vistas of Opportunities

9.1 ASSISTANCES FOR SMALL ENTERPRISES

Government of India and State governments have setup a number of agencies throughout the country to help entrepreneurs in solving technical, infrastructural and financial problems.

The DIC program was launched to provide a number of assistance programs and now acts as nodal agency for implementation of IRDP, TRYSEM and SEEVY programs of self-employment. The SIDO provides a wide range of facilities and services, which include consultancy in techno-economic managerial aspects, training, common facility, services and testing facilities. These services are provided through a network of institutes. The NSIC and SSIC offer indirect financial assistances to small-scale industries in the shape of supply of machinery on hire purchase basis on installments. Registration with NSIC held small-scale industries is needed to take part in government purchase program. The NABARD is an apex organization entrusted with the responsibility concerning policy, planning and operation in the field of credit for agriculture, small-scale industries, cottage and village industries. NABARD refinance is available to SCB (State Cooperative Bank), SRDB and RRB. The IDBI acts as a reservoir from which SFC, SCB and other financial institutions can borrow. The bank also arranges technical or administrative assistance to new units. The SCB is empowered to sanction composite term loan for equipment or working capital or both. The SFC is empowered to grant financial assistance to medium, small and cottage industries. Assistances extended by various agencies are shown below in detail.

Agency/Institution	Nature of Assistance
C & SSI and DIC	Direction for setting up small scale units, Idea on product selection, raw materials, market survey, preparation of project reports, SSI registration, sanction of margin money, subsidies and incentives, market facilities, export and import facilities.
SISI	Identification of products, guidance for project preparation, Vetting of

	projects, guidance for selection of plant and machinery, raw materials, market survey, marketing and special training facilities.
IDBI	Guidelines on large scale and small-scale industry.
IRBI	Rehabilitation assistance.
WBSIDB	Soft loan assistance guidance for industry refinance.
WBFC	Counselling and Guidance, Term loan for acquisition of land, building, plant and machinery, furniture and fixtures, seed capital. Post-disbursement monitoring and assistance.
Nationalized Banks	Term Loans, working capital loan, councelling and Guidance.
NABARD	Financing agriculture, small industries, handicrafts and other non-farm activities.
WBSIC	Hire purchase of plant and machinery.
WBIIDC	Allotment of industrial land and shed.
NSIC	Hire purchase of plant and machinery, securing purchase orders from government departments, prototype development, training.
WBSEB	Power Connection
WBCO	Guidance for setting up small industries, project report preparation, techno economic viability study.
SIDA	Economic viability study and one window clearance.
WB Electronic Dev. Corpn.	Vetting for electronic projects, information on electronics and guidance.
WB Ceramic Dev Corpn.	Information on ceramics.
WB Leather Ind. Dev. Corpn.	Information on leather.
WB Handicrafts Dev. Corpn.	Information on handicrafts.
Tourism Dev Corpn. of WB	Information on tourism and hotel industry.
State Trading Corporation	Marketing assistance.
MMTC	Imports
WB Mineral Dev. & Trading Corpn.	R&D facilities.
WB Handloom & Powerloom Dev. Corpn.	Registration and information on handloom and powerloom projects.
Director, Fruit Processing Govt. of WB	Information on fruit processing and training assistance.
Director, Drug Control	Information on pharmaceuticals.
Directorate of Commercial Taxes	Sales Tax.
WB Pollution Control Board	Pollution Control.

9.1.1 Item, Scope and Scale of Incentives

Any new or existing unit going in for substantial expansion will receive **'Subsidy'** from the government of India in certain areas, such as:

1. Consultancy services
2. Rent for sheds
3. Rent on land
4. Fixed capital investment
5. Power generating set
6. Cost on transformer/power line
7. Consumption of power
8. Interest on term loans
9. Interest on composite loans
10. Interest on working capital loan
11. Rebate on raw materials
12. Special employment
13. Stamp duty and registration fees
14. Return of Octoroi/entry tax
15. Return of Sales Tax as interest free loan as sales tax holiday
16. Deferment of Sales Tax
17. Addition of subsidy for special categories
18. Conversion to piped coal gas.

For the purpose of central investment subsidy, the backward areas of the country have been classified into three categories: A, B and C. The amount of subsidy admissible to small industries in these three categories of areas are as follows:

CATEGORY A: 25% fixed capital investment subject to ceiling of Rs. 25 lakhs.
CATEGORY B: 15% fixed capital investment subject to ceiling of Rs. 15 lakhs.
CATEGORY C: 10% fixed capital investment subject to ceiling of Rs. 10 lakhs.

9.1.2 Role of Banks/Financial Institutions

Banks and financial institutions have played a pioneering role in assisting small-scale industries since 1956.

1. General eligibility criteria for availing of financial assistance from the bank/financial institutions, the unit must satisfy the following:

   (*a*) It should be a small-scale industry as defined by the government from time to time.
   (*b*) Items, that are proposed to be manufactured by the unit, are not in the list of banned items, declared by the government from time to time.
   (*c*) The unit should possess the statutory license/approval for setting up the industry.
   (*d*) Proprietor/partner/director of the unit should have proven integrity and ability to manufacture and sell the product.
   (*e*) The project should be technically feasible and economically viable.

2. Some guidelines for preparation of a scheme/project will be available from the bank/financial institution.
3. Consultancy service for small-scale units are given by the bank/financial institutions. No charges are levied for services rendered.

9.2 ROLE OF NATIONAL SMALL INDUSTRY CORPORATION (N.S.I.C)

The following assistances are extended by the N.S.I.C.

1. Supply of Machinery under hire purchases;
2. Modernisation;
3. Leasing of Machines;
4. Raw material assistance under marketing assistance scheme;
5. Government stores purchase under single point Registration Programme.

N.S.I.C. participate in purchases made by public sector undertaking. They collect orders and then farm out to S.S.I. units. N.S.I.C. also Participates in Foreign Exhibitions.

Under raw materials assistance scheme, scarce raw materials are arranged for S.S.I. units. Unit should be S.S.I. registered units. N.S.I.C. purchase entire raw materials and pay the sells, the raw materials being kept in the Godown of the unit. Imported Pigs are supplied by N.S.I. to Foundary units.

For leasing scheme the units must be:

(*a*) Permanent SSI Regd. Unit;
(*b*) Viable unit;
(*c*) Value of machines not below Rs. 1 lac;
(*d*) Lease rental @2% per month;
(*e*) Rental are Revenue expenditure which go to Tax Benefit;
(*f*) First rental payable after 3 months.

Suggestions and guidelines for S.S.I. units are available from the N.S.I.C.

9.3 STATE FINANCIAL CORPORATIONS

The Industrial Finance Corporation of India was set up to offer financial assistance to only large and medium-sized undertakings. Therefore, need for separate state level development banks which could cater to financial needs of small and medium-sized industrial concerns was rightly felt. Accordingly, the State Financial Corporation Act was passed by Parliament on September 28, 1951, as an enabling measure, under which State Financial Corporations (SFCs) could be set up. The first SFC was set up in Punjab in 1953. Subsequently in other States too, SFCs were set up. At present there are, in all, 18 SFCs in the country. Normally, operations of SFCs are confined to their respective States. However, in some cases they extend to neighbouring States or Union Territories.

Function and Types of Assistance: The SFCs have been set up to extend long-term finance to small and medium-scale industrial undertakings organised as public and private companies, cooperatives, partnerships or proprietary concerns. The SFCs render assistance in the following forms:

1. Grant of loans and advances to industrial concerns for periods not exceeding 20 years;
2. Subscription to debentures repayable within a periods of 20 years;
3. Guarantee of loans raised in the market or from scheduled or cooperative banks by the industrial concerns and repayable within 20 years;
4. Guarantee of deferred payments for purchases of plant, machinery, etc. within India;
5. Underwriting the issue of stocks, shares, bonds and debentures by industrial undertakings.

Apart from independently rendering financial assistance in the above mentioned forms, the SFCs can also act as agent of all the Central and State governments, the Industrial Development Bank of India, the Industrial Finance Corporation of India or some other special industrial financing institution in respect of grant of loan or advances or subscription to bonds or debentures.

Financial resources of SFCs. The resources of SFCs consist of

(*a*) Capital and reserves,
(*b*) Bond and debenture issue,
(*c*) Borrowings from the Reserve Bank of India, the State governments and finance from the Industrial Development Banks of India, and
(*d*) Fixed deposits.

As far as SFC bonds and debentures are concerned, they are mostly subscribed by commercial banks, the Life Insurance Corporation of India and other financial institutions. They are presently an important source of the resource of the SFCs and account for about 30 per cent of them.

The SFCs also borrow from the reserve bank, the State governments and the IDBI. The borrowings of the SFCs including the bond issues at any time should not exceed 10 times of their paid up capital and reserves. During recent year, refinance from IDBI has become the most important source of funds for the SFCs.

Lending Operation of SFCs. The SFCs had started their operations on a modest scale and their lending were rather small in the early years of their existence. So much so that until March 1975, their cumulative loan sanctions aggregated only Rs. 437 crores. Their loans and advances picked up thereafter in a big way. For example in 1990-91 alone, the total assistance sanctioned by SFCs touched the figure of Rs. 1,870 crores.

The SFCs were established to provide financial assistance to small and medium enterprises. Since the concept of small unit has changed over the years, it is some what difficult to determine quantitatively how much financial assistance has been provided to small enterprises. But there is enough evidence to suggest that in the early year of their existence most of SFCs preferred assistance to medium enterprises. In 1966 a beginning of the change in their approach was seen, when they decided to provide a large amount of their loans to small enterprises. Now there is a clear shift in their lending policies in favour of small units in the total sanctions of all SFCs had risen to 82 per cent in 1985-86.

An important aspect of the SFCs' lending policy is assistance to industrial enterprises located in backward areas. For instance, the share of backward areas in the total cumulative assistance sanctioned by all SFCs stood at 45.5 per cent up to March end 1982. During 1985-86, the share of backward areas in total assistance sanctioned by SFCs stood at 53 per cent (Rs. 532.9 crores out of Rs. 1,009.1 crores). This is in conformity with the national policy, which attempts to reduce regional disparities. The SFCs have worked out a scheme of concessional financial assistance to industrial units located in backward areas with the purpose of inducing industrial activity in these regions. In terms of this scheme, industrial concerns in backward regions set soft loans at concessional rates, lower margins, reduced service charges, and so on. The impact of these measures is now visible as industries are now being set up at places where none would have otherwise taken any initiative.

9.4 SMALL INDUSTRIES DEVELOPMENT BANK OF INDIA

With a view to ensuring large flow of financial and non-financial assistance of the small-scale sector, the Government of India announced in the budget for 1988-89, its decision to establish Small Industries Development Bank of India (SIDBI) as a subsidiary of IDBI. The SIDBI Act was passed by the parliament in October 1989 and the bank commenced its operations from April 2, 1990. The immediate thrust of SIDBI will be on:

(*a*) initiating steps for technological upgradation and modernization of existing units;

(*b*) Expanding the channels for marketing the products of SSI sector in domestic and overseas markets; and

(*c*) Promotion of employment oriented industries especially in semi-urban area to create more employment opportunities and there by checking migration of population to higher order urban centers and metropolitan cities.

Financial Resources of SIDBI. The authorised capital of SIDBI is Rs. 250 crores with an enabling provision to increase it to Rs. 1,000 crores. As provided in the Act, SIDBI has taken over the outstanding portfolio of IDBI relating to small-scale sector as of March 31, 1990. The value of such assets taken over by SIDBI is over Rs. 4,000 crores.

Financial Assistance by SIDBI. The financial assistance by SIDBI to the small-scale unit scattered throughout the country is channelised through the existing credit delivery system comprising State Financial Corporations, State Industrial Development Corporations, Commercial Banks, Cooperative Banks and Regional Rural Banks. The total financial assistance sanctioned by SIDBI in 1990-91 was Rs. 1,629 crores of which Rs. 1,508 crores were disbursed.

9.5 SMALL INDUSTRIES SERVICE INSTITUTE (SISI)

Introduction

Training constitutes the mainstay of the extension services provided by SIDO-pre-planned and executed throughout the year in a systematic manner. It is imparted by the network of Small Industries Service Institutes (SISIs) branch institutes, Extension/Production

Centres in the country. There are 26 SISIs, 32 branch Institutes, 40 extension centers scattered all over the country.

Objective

The main objective of the various training programmes conducted by SISI's is to upgrade the skills of workers as well as the managerial capabilities of their management personal. EDP programmes are also conducted to convert certain categories of persons in to prospective entrepreneurs and to enable them to set up their own Small Scale units. Apart from imparting training, SISIs also provide technical service in specialized fields to small-scale entrepreneurs.

Training Programmes

The following are the different types of training programmes conducted by SIDO through SISIs:

Training in Industrial management

These courses are designed for small entrepreneurs and supervisors engaged in managerial duties. These training programmes are conducted in the evening at places of concentration of SSIs. The SISIs do not charge any fee for conducting these courses expecting the courses conducted at Bombay, Calcutta, New Delhi, Madras, Ahmedabad, Bangalore, Pune, Kanpur, Ludhiana and Hyderabad. The following management courses are conducted:

(*a*) Industrial Management Course;
(*b*) Specialised courses in Management;
(*c*) Techno-Managerial courses;
(*d*) Ad-hoc courses in management subjects.

Technical Training courses

Regular and Ad-hoc training courses in various technical trades are conducted by the SISIs, Extension/Production centers for workers both skilled and semi-skilled, sponsored by the SSIs for improving their skills and broadening their areas of competence to meet the specific requirements of small scale industries. Trainees of these courses are paid regular stipend of Rs. 100-00 per month. The following types of technical courses are conducted:

(*a*) Shop practice courses (6 months - full time)
(*b*) Trade oriented courses (6 months - full time)
(*c*) Process oriented courses (3-6 months - full time)
(*d*) Product oriented courses (3-6 months - full time)
(*e*) Blue print reading courses (part time evening courses)
(*f*) Ad-hoc courses (short duration of 1-3 months).

All India Courses

Regular full time courses of all India importance are conducted at the following centers:

Training in the manufacture of Thermometers, Glass blowing and Scientific apparatus is imparted in the institutes at Solan and Bangalore.

Training/Demonstration through mobile workshop

Mobile workshops are attached to some of the SISs which visit the areas of concentration of artisans in a particular field and provide demonstration and training in these fields. These mobile vans impart training/demonstration primarily in subjects like Blacksmithy, Carpentry, Sheet metal, Potter, Leather, Glass Blowing, General Engineering etc.

9.6 THE NATIONAL BANK FOR AGRICULTURE AND RURAL DEVELOPMENT (NABARD)

The National Bank for Agriculture and rural development (NABARD) was established by an act of Parliament, 1981 and it came into existence on 12th July 1982 for financing agriculture, Small Scale industries, cottage and village industries, handicraft, rural crafts and other allied economic activities in rural areas for promoting integrated rural development and securing prosperity of rural areas. It is an apex organisation entrusted with the responsibility concerning policy. Planning and operations in the field of credit for agriculture and non farms activities. NABARD's refinance is available to state Land Development Banks (SLDBs), State Co-operatives Banks (SCBs), schedule Commercial Banks (SCBs) and Regional Rural Banks (RRBs) while the ultimate beneficiaries of investment credit can be individuals, partnership concerns, companies, state owned corporations or co-operative Societies. It operates in the country through its 12 regional offices located in the State capitals of all major States and Sub-offices.

9.7 INDUSTRIAL DEVELOPMENT BANK OF INDIA (IDBI)

Object

The Industrial Development Banks of India was set up on July 1, 1964. The Bank is intended to serve as a reservoir from which the existing financial Institutions can draw. It seeks to cover the gaps left by the various scheduled banks in the field of Industrial Finance. It promotes the establishment of new enterprise especially in key industries and assist projects both in the private and public sector.

Recourses

The bank is empowered to borrow from the market by issuing its own bonds and debenture from the Reserve Bank of India. The bank is also empowered to borrow from any other authority or institution with prior consent of the Government of India. It can borrow foreign currency from any bank and can accept deposits from the public for a minimum of 12 months as also any gifts and donations. All loans, gifts, donations and grants are credited to a Development Assistance fund which are utilized for granting assistance to concerns which can not raise their requirements from other sources.

Functions

The bank is expected to combine commercial, promotional and re-financing activities. It will subscribe to or buy stocks, shares, bonds or debenture of the S.F.C or any other Scheduled Bank/financial institutions. The bank can arrange technical or administrative assistance of any industrial concern or person for promotion, management or expansion of any industry. It will also plan, promote and develop industries to cover the gaps in the existing capital structure. The bank may also undertake research and survey for evaluating or dealing with marketing or investments.

Upto 1976, the IDBI functioned as a wing of the Reserve Bank of India. To enable it to play a more dynamic role in promoting the growth of industries, it was delinked from the RBI. It now functions as an autonomous institution under the control of the Government of India, having a separate board of directors, fully professionalised and specialized in three areas:

(*a*) Assessment of project
(*b*) Monitoring at the stage of construction
(*c*) Ensuring healthy functioning of the unit to serve the overall national interest.

9.8 REGIONAL RURAL BANK (RRB)

The Regional Rural Bank came into being as a result of measures undertaken under the 20 point economic programme announced by the Government of India in the year 1975. The first five RRBs were established on 2nd October, 1975. The main objectives of the RRBs are briefly summarised as follows:

(*a*) Taking the banking services to the doorsteps of rural masses, particularly in unbanked rural areas.
(*b*) Making available institutional credit to the weaker sections of the society who had little access to cheaper loans and had been depending on private money lenders.
(*c*) Mobilise rural saving and channelise them for supporting productive activities in the rural areas.
(*d*) To create a supplementary channel for the flow of credit from the Central Money Market to the rural areas.

Since 1975, there has been a rapid expansion in the number of RRBs as on 31st December 1986 was 194 covering 351 district of the country. The regional rural banks are to provide credit facilities to the rural poor in general and the small and marginal farmers, agriculture labourers, rural artisans and small entrepreneur in particular. Although the nationalized commercial banks have been assigned the task of extending credit facilities to such sections of the people in rural area, but it was felt necessary to channelise the credit flow in these sections through a particular source which can be simultaneously capable of mobilising the rural savings for rural development.

9.9 SCHEDULED COMMERCIAL BANK

Consequent to their nationalization, commercial banks have adopted various promotional measures to sanction credit to the small industries sector. The reserve bank of India has issued instructions that no worthwhile proposals of the small units would be rejected on conditions of lack of adequate security. Another important directive of the RBI relates to the reduction of the period of scrutiny of loan applications.

The branch managers are empowered to take maximum number of credit decision at their level. The intention is that credits limits upto Rs. 25000=00 and those exceeding this amount upto Rs. 2 Lakhs may be normally disposed off within a period of 4 weeks and 8-9 weeks respectively from the date of receipt of the application.

Special measure have been undertaken by the banks to increase the flow of funds particularly to village, tiny and cottage units at specified rates of interest. The bank credit to such industries would be treated as composite term loan for equipment or working capital or both upto Rs. 25000 with repayment period of 7-10 years or more. Simplified interview cum appraisal forms for small units have been prescribed and disposal of these small loan proposals is carried out within a period of 30 days at district level itself.

The commercial banks have also liberalized their procedures for advances to the units in the small scale sector through introduction of a slab system of rat of interest and creation of an equity fund for SSI. The banks are also providing consultancy services to the Small Scale units.

9.10 SOME EXPORT PROMOTION COUNCILS

1. Engineering Export Promotion Council, 14-1/B Ezra Street, 3rd floor, Calcutta-700001.
2. Chemicals & Allied products Export Promotion Council, 2nd floor, 14/1B, Ezra street, Calcutta-700001.
3. Chemicals, Pharmaceuticals & Cosmetics Export Promotion Council, Jhanshi Castle (4th floor), 7 Coorperage Road Bombay-400 001.
4. Plastics & Linoleum Export Promotion Council, 612/615, Tulsiani Chambers, Backbay Reclamation, Nariman Point, Bombay-400021.
5. Leather Export Promotion Council, Marble Hall, 3/8, Vepery High Road, Madras-3.
6. Sports Goods Export Promotion Council, IE/6, Jhandewalan Extension, New Delhi-110055.
7. Marine products Export Development Authority, 'World Trade Center', Mahatma Gandhi Road, P.B. No. 1708, Ernakulam, South Cochin.
8. Processed foods Export Promotion Council, 105 New Delhi, House, 27, Barakhamba Road, New Delhi-110001.
9. Spices Export Promotion Council, 'World Trade Center', M.G. Road, Ernakulam-6.
10. Cash EW Export Promotion Council 'World Trade Center', M.G. Road, Ernakulam-6.
11. Wool and Woolens Export Promotion Council, 612/714, Askoke Estate, Barakamba Road, New Delhi-110001.
12. Cotton Textiles Export Promotion Council, Engineering Center, 5th floor, 9, Mathew Road, Bombay-400004.
13. Silk Rayon Textiles Export Promotion Council, Reshan Bhavan, 78, Veer Nariman Road, Bombay-400004.
14. Shellac Export Promotion Council, 'World Trade Center', 14-1/B Ezra Street, Calcutta-700001.

15. Apparels Export Promotion Council, Sahyog Building 4th floor 58, Nehru Place, New Delhi-110019.
16. Mica Trading Corporation, 137 Patliputra Colony, Patna-800013.

9.11 OTHER ORGANISATIONS

1. Federation of India Export Organisations, PHD House, 4/2 Siri Institutional Area, Hauz Khas, New Delhi-110016.
2. Trade Development Authority, Bank of Baroda Building, 16, Parliament Street, New Delhi-110001.
3. State Trading Corporation of India Ltd., Chandralok, 36, Janpath, New Delhi 110001.
4. Minerals & Metal Trading Corporation, Express Building, Bahadurshah Zafar Marg, New Delhi-110021.
5. Export Credit & Guarantee Corporation, Express Towers, P.O. Box 373, Nariman Point, Bombay-400021.
6. National Small Industries Corporation, Okhla Industrial Estate, New Delhi.
7. Export Inspection Council, Pragati Towers, 26, Rajendra Place, New Delhi.
8. Indian Institute Foreign Trade, Ashok Bhawan, 93, Nehru Place, New Delhi-19.

Appendices

1. BUSINESS MANAGEMENT TERMINOLOGIES

Accountability: Responsibility for results.
Accounting: The system of keeping records of financial transactions and of summarizing these data in appropriate reports for management, financial institutions, or government agencies.
Administer: To manage, especially in a setting that emphasizes the application of fixed procedures and minimal environmental turbulence.
Administrators: Person who administer. Also a title use for some managerial positions such as the administration of a hospital.
Advertising and promotion specialist: A person well-versed in the cost and appropriateness of different modes of advertising and promoting a product or service and thereby able to advise on the best means to use in generating interest in the product or service.
Affiliate: A company that works closely with another company in serving a particular market. A subsidiary of a multinational corporation that services a country other than the larger company's home country is an affiliate.
Allocate: To divide resources among competing interests. Allocating financial resources through a budgetary process is a prime example of such division. Other resources such as people and time are allocated by some mechanism if there are varying ways to employ them.
Allocation: A quantity of resource allocated for a particular item. In speaking about money, a travel allocation would be an amount of money set aside for travel.
Analytical methods: Methods of analysis that use mathematics and logic to resolve managerial problems Financial ratio analysis and operations research analysis are prime examples of analytical methods.
Antitrust legislation: Laws that prohibit the formation and operation of business monopolies. The Sherman Antitrust law is the best of American antitrust law.
Appraise: To assess the value of a property, a person's job performance, or other item of value.

Assessment center: A method of evaluating candidates for a managerial position that involves bringing the candidates to a central location for a series of tests, interviews, and exercises. Assessors evaluate the candidates' performance and make recommendations to the person or persons who will make the final choice.
Assets: The item of value owned by a company or a person. Also the items fitting this description that appear on the left-hand side of a balance sheet opposite the liabilities.
Authority: The right to use assigned resources within one's discretion to accomplish an assigned task, including the right to direct people and other resources. Authority is always limited by the organization's policies and procedures and the rules of the larger society.
Automation: The system of production that uses self-controlled machines to accomplish the task at hand. When future self controlled devices are incorporated, one say that there is greater automation in the process.
Autonomy: The ability to operate independently of other units. A manager may have great autonomy in his job, or one can speak of a subsidiary of a conglomerate having limited autonomy.

Balance of payments: The payments due a country for exports less the payments it owes for imports during a particular time period. The notion can be applied to a single pair of countries or to one country versus all others. The term "balance of trade" is also used.
Bankrupt: A legal or economic term that means insolvency or inability to pay one's debts.
Basic strategy objective: A company or organization's central aim in trying to achieve its overall financial or other objectives. For example, Sears and Roebuck's basic strategy objective during its early decades was to merchandise true values to farmers and their families through mail-order merchandising.
Behavioural psychology: The school of psychology that relies exclusively on the analysis of empirically observed behaviour in accounting for why people act as they do.
Behavioral science approach to management: The school of through that gives primary importance to the disciplines of psychology, sociology, and anthropology in explaining management and in trying to improve the practice of management.
Billing: The business function of giving customers or clients formal notice for payment is due on a certain date for goods or services provided.
Boss: The person in charge or holding final authority.
Brand name product: A product sold with a company's name or other specific name attached to it rather than being sold with only a generic name.
Break Even point: The level of sales or production that is necessary to break even—that is, to lose no money and to make no money. Analysis whose objective is to determine this level is called break-even analysis.
Budget: An approval scheme that specifies how much is to be spent on each category of expenditure during a given time period. The scheme is usually compiled in a document referred to as the budget.
Budget allocation: The amount to be spent in a particular category as specified in a budget.
Budgeting: The process of developing a budget.

Budget-based institution: An organization that receives relatively assured income rather than being subject to an immediately responsive market. Government agencies and nonprofit organizations are example of such institutions.
Buying-in: The process of getting approval to provide a product or service by underestimating the total cost.
By product: A substance, product, or condition produced by a production process in addition to the primary item produced.

Capacity: The maximum amount of product or service that could be provided by a giving mechanism.
Capital: Wealth that an organisation possesses to employ in achieving its aims.
Capital equipment: A Company or organization's equipment or buildings whose purchase required the expenditure of substantial capital.
Capital formation: The process by which capital is created in an economy.
Capital-intensive industry: An industry that in comparison to other industries requires large investments of capital per dollar of sales or production. Frequently contrasted with labour-intensive industry.
Capital investment: A investment or an employing of a company's capital in a specific project.
Capital investment decisions: Decisions regarding the employment of a firm's capital. Since capital is usually invested in plant or equipment for long periods, it is of utmost importance that decisions be made with as much knowledge as possible about the expected rate of return on the capital. Thus there is a vest body of literature on this kind of analysis and decision making.
Carrying costs: The costs incurred by holding inventory.
Centralization: A method of organizing that concentrates decision making at the top of organization's hierarchy.
Client: A customer of a service-producing enterprise.
Commander: A person empowered to give orders and expect results, most frequently in military context.
Committee: A group of people assigned to perform a given task as a group.
Common Market: The group of Western European countries banded together to provide a larger market open to all members, or any market formed in this manner.
Communication: The transfer of meaning from one (the sender) to another (the receiver). The sender and receiver may be persons, corporate entities, or other group of people.
Compensation: That which is given in exchange for work performed. Compensation is usually money but may include other items such as privileges.
Competition: The companies that are alternative sources of supply for a given company's customer or clients.
Computer: Electronic device that can perform multiple complex calculation or logic operation.
Computer program: An integrated set of instructions for a computer to use in performing a particular task.

Computer programmer: A person who creates computer programs.
Conflict: Disagreements or clashes in feelings within an organization.
Conglomerate: A company made up of many other companies in a wide variety of industry. Many such companies were formed in the late 1960s.
"Conscience" activities: The activities directed to give in vision and to setting standards and auditing performance against them.
Constituencies: The various interest groups who vie for the attention of an organization. Faculty, students, parents, foundations, and Government agencies such constitute a constituency for a university.
Consumer: The person who is the user of the product or service produced.
Consumerism: The social movement that insists that products and services be of unassailable quality and without any possible hazardous side affects.
Control: The management function that aims to keep activities directed in such a way that desired results are achieved. Monitoring of performs is the starting point of all control. In case performance deviates from what is expected, corrected action must be taken to get the process back on the track.
Cooperation: Joint effort to achieve a desired result.
Coordinate: To integrate one's own efforts with those of others to achieve a desired result. Frequently one speaks of coordination of efforts in various parts of the organization so that a manager is coordinating his efforts with those of people in other departments.
Corporation: A legal entity formed by persons to enter a business while limiting their liability to the moneys they have contributed to the enterprise.
Cost accountant: An account whose primary responsibility is to determine the cost of goods or services. The cost figures are to be used in determining profit levels and in meeting other demands for judgments on what the costs are.
Cost center: In a business, costs are either assigned exclusively to the business as a whole, or the business is broken into parts each of which is responsible for certain costs. In the latter event, the parts are cost centers. In a multidivision company, the divisions may be the cost center.
Cost effectiveness analysis: The method of analysis that compares the cost of alternative solutions for a problem with the relative benefits provided by each.
Cost of capital: The rate of return that should be used as the minimum acceptable for considering a given capital expenditure; the "rental" cost of money. Thus, projects must pay more than it would cost to "rent" the money required, or no financial benefit has been produced.
Credit: Ability to borrow funds, or the funds so borrowed.
Critical path analysis: A method of analysing the scheduling of a project with multiple subactivities. The method uses network diagram that represent the component activities. Time required to complete each activity is analyzed, and the earliest and latest beginning date for each activity is specified. Finally the longest path through the sequence of activities (the critical path) is identified, and that path receives special attention so that the project will be completed on time.
Customers: The persons or organizations that consume the product or services provided by another company.

Data processing: The function of handling the masses of data involved in the multiple transactions related to a firm's business. Since most large firms use computers in this Function, the department in charge of the computing is frequently called the Data Processing Department. Similarly, the function is often referred to as Electronic Data Processing (EDP).
Decentralization: A method of organizing that disburses decision making to multiple locations and levels rather than concentrating it at the organization hierarchy.
Decision: A determination to take a particular action.
Decision making: The process of arriving at decisions.
Decision theory: A body of analytical tools including logic, mathematical models (especially models that use probability theory), and diagrams to be used in decision-making.
Decision tree: From decision theory, a diagram that looks very much like a tree and that allows alternative decisions to be pictured in an orderly fashion.
Deficit: The amount by which expenses exceed the funds available (or allocated) to cover them.
Delegation: The process a manager uses to assign a task or part of a task to one of his subordinates.
Demand pattern: The relative distribution of demand among the various markets served or that could be served.
Demographics: The study of populations as regards their numbers, birth, death, etc., and the statistics so produced.
Department: A basic subunit of an organization, frequently used in the formal title of some subunits.
Departmentalization: The process of grouping organizational activities into basic subunits, usually done using a common characteristic such as function, product, or geography.
Depreciate: The process by which the worth or equipment or buildings are assigned decreased value due to deterioration, obsolescence, or other considerations.
Depression: A period of extremely low business, marked by high unemployment and extreme declines in demand.
Developed countries: Those countries with the highest standard of living, generally the industrialised nations.
Developing countries: Nations that have begun to industrialize but whose economics are still dominated by small farms and low personal-income levels.
Direct labor cost: The cost that is attributable to the production process itself and that is so ascribed in accounting for the results of the business. Direct labor costs are frequently contrasted with indirect labor costs, which are costs counted in determining results but are not part of the production payroll.
Direct: To indicate that a certain action should be taken to command.
Discounted cash flow analysis: The method of allowing a stream of fund flows that are to occur over a period of years to be summarized in to a single number show that alternative streams can be compared.
Distribution: The function of dispensing the goods manufactured or warehoused to the locations where they will be consumed or received by customer. Choices of modes of

transportation to be used and there timeliness and costs are important elements of the distribution function.

Distributive system: The mechanism setup to accomplish the distribution task.

Distributor: A company or business agent between the manufacture and the end user.

Dividend: The amount of profit for a given period returned to the owner of one share of a companies stock.

Division of labor: The method of dividing a task into specialized subtasks with different people doing different subtasks so that they may become very efficient at performing there subtask and there by contribute to accomplishing the overall job at least cost.

Economic development: The process by which a nation's economy grows and moves toward providing its people a higher standard of living.

Economic Viability: Means:

1. Market: Region proposed to be covered. If market survey done, copy to be enclosed: (a) Major competitors in the field. (b) Competitive edge in terms of price, quality, publicity, sales campaign etc.
2. Selling Arrangements: Sales, organizational setup, appointment of sales representatives, and machinery for collecting bills. If sales is arranged through distributors/sole agents, their names and address, their experience, organizational setup, commission payable, credit period of contract, advance payment if to be made.

Econometric methods: Methods used by a branch of economics that makes extensive use of mathematical modelling and simulation.

EDP (electronic data processing): Data processing using computer.

Effective demand: The demand that will be realized if the product or service is made available.

Effectiveness: The extent to which the desired result is realized. Frequently compared with efficiency.

Efficiency: Output divided by input, or the extent to which the result produced was produced at least cost.

Employee satisfaction: The degree to which employee needs are met, a relative measure.

Entrepreneur: A person who starts and develops a business.

Environment: The external setting in which a business operates. Of special importance are the factors that may have a large impact on the business's success—such factors as competition, labour market conditions, the general economic climate, government regulation, etc.

Equipment: Machinery and devices that can be employed in producing the results the firms desire.

Executive: A manager. Most frequently used to refer to middle and upper levels of the organizational hierarchy.

Exports: Goods and services provided from one country to another. Generally contrasted with imports, goods consumed in a home country but produced abroad.

Extrapolation: A method of forecasting that assumes that the future will continue to reflect already established trends.

Facilities: Buildings and structure that can be used in a firm's operations.
Factors of production: The elements necessary in order to produce goods and services in an economic, for example capital and labor.
Federal decentralization: A mode of organizing a large multidivision company by decentralizing authority and centralizing control.
Feedback mechanism: A mechanism to allow recognition of unexpected deviations in a process and prompt corrective action so that the process will stay at the level needed to obtain the desired results.
First-line supervisor: A manager who supervises other employees at the lowest managerial level in the organizational hierarchy. These people are also referred to as first-line management.
Fixed capital: Money invested permanently in building, machinery, and equipment.
Fixed costs: Costs that are incurred regardless of the level of production. Frequently contrasted with variable costs, which depend on the amount produced.
Financial projection: 1. Projection of performance and profitability.
2. Break even analysis.
3. Details relating to the assumptions on which the projection on profitability have been made.
4. Assessment and computation of working capital.
Forecasting: Estimating the value of a certain variable in the future, such as sales for the coming year.
Foreman: A manager who is in charge of one of the basic units of a production facility.
Formal organization: The structure that indicates to whom each person in the hierarchy reports, frequently diagrammed in an "organization chart".
Free enterprise system: The economic system that has private ownership of property and business units operated with a minimum of governmental interference.
Functional authority: Authority based on a business function whose exercise may require compliance by persons who are not subordinates of the person exercising the authority. For example, a purchasing department may require person in another department to follow its procedures for ordering equipment.
Function organization: A mode of organizing a business that makes the manufacturing, selling, engineering, accounting, and other departments defined by business functions the basic sub unit of the organization.

Gantt chart: A chart to be used in planning and coordinating an activity that involves several parallel subactivities. A time line is depicted horizontally at the top of the chart. Below the time line are horizontal bars for each activity, which the length of each bar representing its duration and the left-end border representing the beginning time of the activity.
Goals: The basic aims of enterprise.
Gross National Product (GNP): The sum of the values of all the products and services produced by a national economy during a single year.

Hierarchy of needs: A construct in Maslow's theory of motivation. The theory postulates that human needs consist of the hierarchy: physiological, security affiliation, esteem, and self-actualization needs. The theory suggest that the lower-level needs must be satisfied before higher-order needs come into play and that once lower-level needs are satisfied, they lose their motivational importance.

Human asset accounting: A set of method for trying to value a firm's human resources.

Human relations approach to management: An approach to management thought and practice that insists on the primacy of the relations among a firm's employees as the determinant of success.

Hygiene and housekeeping activities: Activities that do not contribute to the basic result of the business but that is done poorly could damage the business, for example keeping the premises clean, the employees fed, reporting to the government etc.

Hygiene Factors: A construct in Herzberg's theory of motivation, factors that do not motivate positively but that could demotivate if handled poorly.

Impact: The consequences an action has in addition to those that constitute its raison d'etre, for example an action taken in one department may have consequences far beyond that department, or a production process may have polluting wastes as an impact.

Incentives: The items provided as "carrots" using a carrot-stick theory of motivation.

Industrial anthropology: The science of man in the work place. Concepts of sociology, psychology, and physiology are applied to understanding life in an industrial setting.

Industrial Engineer: An engineer who applies scientific methods to solving work related problems, especially in a factory or production setting.

Industrial Engineering: The discipline that includes the scientific principals and research the industrial engineer applies in the work place.

Industrial physiology: The subdivision of physiology that is concerned with the impact of specific industrial practices on the human body and its functioning.

Industrial psychology: The branch of psychology that studies human behaviour in organizational settings, with special attention being given to behaviour in business firms.

Industrial relations: A approach to management promoted by some behavioral scientists. The central theme is the relief or prevention of dissatisfaction among employees.

Industrial sociology: The study of human institutions and groups and there operating characteristics in an industrial setting.

Information: Facts or data that can be communicated.

Inflation: The process by which money losses some of its value.

Inflationary pressures: Economic conditions that if left unchecked will bring on inflation, for example continued wage increases unmatched by productivity improvements.

Individual professional contributors: Managerial personal who may supervise no one (except possibly a secretary and assistant) but who make major contributions to the results of the firm by applying their professional competence, for example an advertising specialist.

Information organization: The set of relationships that reflect actual interactions within an organization as contrasted with the formal organization structure.

Informal organization: The set of relationships that reflect actual interactions within an organization as contrasted with the formal organization structure.

Innovation: Activity or developments in a firm that result in the adoption of a new product, business, or way of doing things.
Instalment credit: Credit extended in exchange for the promise to repay the money with interest in equal payments at specified intervals until the money is repaid.
Institutional investors: Investors who represent large organizations and as a consequence buy and sell very large blocks of stocks bonds, for example, mutual funds, pension funds, university endowment funds. Since the late 1960s such investors have come to dominate the market, whereas individual investors were once a large part of the market.
Insurance: A method of protecting individuals against the effects of a specific kind of loss by having each individual in the insured group pay a fee in exchange for a promise to be compensated in the event the loss occurs.
Integrate: A process by which a manager meshes his work with that of others (in his unit, in other units, above him, below him, and laterally) in order to ensure performance.
Interest group: A group branded together in order to pursue a particular objective.
Intermediate product: A product made to be used in making another product rather than to be used by an end user, for example a basic chemical product such as carbon dioxide.
Inter personal relations: Relations among people, based on continued face-to-face inter action.
Invention: A technological advance, either a product or a means of doing something.
Inventor: A person who creates or produces an invention.
Inventory: The supply of goods or resources on hand at one time.
Inventory models: Models that may be used to determine when inventories should be resupplied.
Investment: An application of a firm's resources (especially money) in a means that is expected to pay off in future results.
Investment banking: The function performed by financial institutions that underwrite and sell new issues of stocks and bonds of a company and advice the company on such matters.
Investment decision: A decision about how to employ substantial portion of a firm's resources, especially capital.
Investment instruments: Vehicles that may be used to invest funds, for example stocks, bond, mutual funds, certificates for deposit.
Irreversible decision: A decision whose impact cannot be removed or reversed, for example introducing a completely new technology (the secret of the technology cannot be reinstated).

Job description: An exposition of the duties and responsibilities that are inherent in a particular job.
Job enlargement: Including more tasks or more kinds of tasks in a given job in order to make the job more satisfying.
Job enrichment: Changing some aspects of a job in order to have it satisfy more of a person's higher-order needs.
Joint venture: A business venture that is funded by more than one company. For example, the European SST was a joint venture of British and French companies.

Key activities: Activities in the most important business area: marketing innovation, human organisation, financial resources, physical resources, productivity, social responsibility and profit requirements.

Knowledge worker: An employee whose major contribution depends on his employing his knowledge rather than his muscle power and coordination, frequently contrasted with production workers who employ muscle power and coordination to operate machines.

Labour economics: The branch or discipline of economics that concentrates its studies on the supply and demand of labour in an economy.

Labour-intensive industry: An industry that, in comparison to other industries, requires large expenditures for labour per dollar of sales or production. Frequently contrasted with capital-intensive industry.

Labour unions: Organisation of workers banded tighter to promote worker interests, especially higher wages and better fringe benefit and working conditions.

Labour position: Requirement/availability of skilled/unskilled personnel for the unit.

Large scale organisations: Organisation that require huge investments or employ thousands of a worker, as contrasted with small businesses, proprietorship, or businesses with limited managerial employees.

Lateral mobility: Ability to move from one area of a business to another, as from production to sales. Frequently compared to vertical mobility.

Leadership: The managerial function of providing guidance in setting business goals or quality standards.

Lead time: The time that must pass between a decision and its coming to fruition, for example the number of years between the decision to build a new steel mill and the time when it can be placed in operation.

Limited liability insurance: Insurance that covers only certain kinds of losses or only losses of a particular size.

Linear programming: An operation research technique that can be used to determine the proper mix of products or ingredients to maximise profits or some other dimension of interest to management.

Line management job: A managerial job that includes supervision and of the central business function such as selling or production. Frequently contrasted with staff jobs.

Liquidate: To terminate an operation by disposing of all assets an inventory returning the proceeds to the owners of the operation.

Long-range planning: Planning with a multi-year time horizon. Contrasted with yearly plans and other short-range plans.

Logistics: The function of moving, storing and distributing resources goods.

Manage: In an organisation setting, to mobilise resources for the achievement of a human purpose.

Manageability: The characteristic inherent in an organisation that be managed, believed to be related to complexity and size. For example, some commentators have questioned the manageability of large cities.

Management: The group of person who manage an organisation. Also the discipline concerted with understanding and improving the knowledge of how to manage.

Management by objective (MBO) The approach to management that emphasises the central role of objectives for each unit of an organisation and for each individual contributor. The approach emphasises self-control as a consequence of having clear objectives for each individual.

Management Development: The means by which an organisation contributes to the development of the managerial abilities of its management group.

Management science: The approach to management that emphasises the application of scientific methods for the improved understanding and practice of management.

Managers: The people in an organisation whose jobs include managing responsibilities.

Managerial accounting: The accounting done in a firm to produce reports that will contribute to management decisions. Contrasted with tax accounting or financial accounting.

Managerial economics: The subdivision of economic that emphasises notions of direct relevance to managers; decisions such as investment and pricing decisions receive special attention.

Manual Worker: A worker whose primary contribution is a result of his or her muscle power and coordination.

Manufacturing business: A business whose central role is to produce an item, for example, the chemical industry. Manufacturing is frequently contrasted to retailing or to other service industries.

Marginal Costs: The costs of producing and selling an additional unit.

Marginal efficiencies: Efficiencies that if adopted would make very small changes in overall results.

Marginal revenue: The revenue that would be produced by producing and selling an additional unit.

Market: An area in which buyers and sellers may come together or an area of demand (however defined).

Market analysts: Specialists who attempted to define, map, quantify, and develop information about markets.

Market standing: The relative ranks of various firms in a single market, for example first, second, etc.

Market research: The research produced by market analysts.

Mass-distribution system: A system for distributing goods or services to large number of customers who are dispersed within an area.

Mass-production system: A system of production that is geared to produce large numbers of unit.

Matrix organization: A mode of organizing, especially of large technological projects, that includes person having both task and function assignments and as a consequence being attached to two units of the organization at one time (with the possibility of having two bosses). The "matrix" is suggested by a diagram that has functional units across the top and task units down the side with entries indicating person's from various functions assigned to a given task.

Media: Vehicles for communication, for example television radio, newspaper, etc.
Middle managers: Managers who occupy positions in the formal organisation above first-line supervisors and below top managements.
Minimum profitability: The least level of profitability a particular industry should accept in order to take the risk inherent in the industry.
MIS (Management Information System): A term created to describe a management's mechanism for obtaining, processing, storing, retrieving and using information, frequently suggesting the use of computers.
Mission: An organisation's paramount objectives for intermediate future.
Model: A simplified replication of a problem situation that can be manipulated to explore the range and quality of solution to the problem.
Motivation: Personal mechanism that move an individual action.
Multinational corporation: A corporation that has significant production, markets and operations in many countries.
Multiplier impact: An impact that promotes multiples other impacts, as the multiplier impact of the building of infrastructure in a developing nation.
Multi product, multimarket or multi technology company: A company that produces multiple products, operates in many markets, or employs as a wide variety of technologies in its operations.
Mutual fund: An investment vehicles that allows the investor to have an interest in many companies without being the direct owner of their stocks.

Network analysis: Analysis used in planning and scheduling, for example critical path analysis.
Nonmanufacturing business: A business whose primary function is selling or some business function.
Not-for-profit organization: An organization such as a university whose mission is other than to create a profit from its operations.

Objectives: The levels of result to be sought within a specific time period.
Obsolete: No longer in use; outmoded.
Operations: The activities associated with the production of current result. Frequently contrasted with the preparations for future business opportunities.
Operation manager: A manager whose prime responsibility is in operations.
Operation research: The discipline that studies the application of mathematical tools and logic to the solution of industrial problems.
Optimal solution: A solution to a problem that is the best one possible.
Optimization: The process of finding the optimal solution to a management problem usually using an operations research model.
Organization chart: The pictorial representation of the formal organization.
Organization design: The design principle incorporated in the formal organization of a company or the discipline that studies alternative ways to design organizations.
Organization psychology: The branch of psychology that studies human behaviour in organizations; includes industrial psychology.

Organizing: The process of creating a formal organization structure or of breaking a task to be performed into subtasks.
Output: That which results from a production process.

Participative management: An approach to improving management practice that emphasises participation of all impacted parties in decisions.
Partnership: A mode of legally structuring a business that includes specifications of each partner's role and responsibility.
Payback period: The period required for the proceeds from an investment to equal the amount invested.
Payroll: The business function that calculates the amount due each employee and conveys those funds to the employee by check or alternative means.
Pension: A regular amount received by a retired employee based on certain payments made by employer and/or employee during the employees's working years.
Pension fund: The invested proceeds of the funds contributed by an employer and/or employees for the purpose of paying pensions.
Performance: Actual results obtained. Sometimes used to denote the achievement of positive results.
Personal income: Wages and salaries paid to individuals. Frequently contrasted with investment income.
Personnel administration: The management role concern with the hiring and training of employees and with keeping employee records.
Personnel appraisal: The evaluation of employee's performance and interaction between a boss and subordinate to discuss the subordinate's performance and future objectives, a process frequently discussed in conjunction with MBO.
Personnel department: The unit of an organization that performs the personnel administration role.
Personnel management: The management of the firm's human resources. Sometimes called human resources management.
PERT Chart (Program Evaluation Review Technique): A planning technique that uses charts, created by the navy to aid in planning a project and in evaluating progress after it is under way.
Pilot-plant: A plant built to test a new process, usually on a scale much less than that proposed for subsequent implementation. Frequently, a pilot-plant test of a process if successful will suggest ways to improve the larger facility to be built later.
Planed obsolescence: An approach to design that utilises the expectation that the product design will become out of vogue before the product itself is physically unusable; the approach includes subsequent designs that are intended to make previous designs unfashionable. Also, the design of products to become obsolete earlier than necessary in order to be able to introduce new design.
Planning The management function that includes decision and actions to insure future results.
Planning assumptions or hypotheses: Assumptions or hypotheses used in plans.
Plans: The view of the future are specified in the decisions resulting from planning.

Planed: The facilities that a firm can use from production.
Policy: A specified mode of approaching a particular area in the future, for example a marketing policy.
Power: Ability to influence, to make other act in a way desired by the holder of the power.
PPBS (Planning, Programming, Budgeting System): A comprehensive planning methodology utilised by some public agencies.
Priorities: The relative order in which an organization intends to address a list of issues or areas.
Probability mathematics: A subdivision of mathematics that is concerned with modeling situation with outcomes that have relative likelihoods of occurrence.
Procedures: Specified ways to approach narrowly defined situation, for example procedure for recording a sale.
Process industry: An industry that neither manufactures nor provides an intangible service; rather it subject certain resources to a process, for example the oil refining industry.
Producing capital: Capital invested in the land, buildings, and equipment use to produce the product or service.
Product lines: The various basic categories and subcategories of product produce or provided.
Product manager: A managerial role that has responsibility for coordinating all of the activates that effect the results produced from the assigned product. Such a manager might coordinate all of production, advertising, selling and distributing.
Product mix: The variety of products offered by one company.
Productivity: The relative output for given levels of input especially the production per production employee. The continuing challenge is to improve productivity.
Profit: The difference between income and costs.
Profit centers: In large multidivision companies, profits may be calculated in various subdivision of the company to add up to the overall profit, compare with costs centers. A manager in charge of a profit center (one of the subdivision) has profit and loss responsibility.
Programmer: A person who creates computer programs.
Proprietor: The sole owner and manager of a small business.
Prototype: A model of a potential new product, use to evaluate the product's prospect.
Public-service institutions: Institutions such as government and non profit institution which exist to provide a service in a non profit manner.
Purchasing power: The ability a person or a group of people has to purchase goods and services because of their income.

Qualitative factors: Factors to be incorporated in decisions that cannot be quantified such as values and beliefs.
Quality control: The production function that sets quality standards and monitors the production process to ensure that the process yields goods meeting the established standards.
Quality of life: The qualitative assessment of the relative quality of living condition, including attention to pollutants, noise, aesthetics, complexity, etc.

Queing theory: The brunch of management science that uses models of waiting-lines to approximate certain industrial problem situations.

Ratio analysis: Financial analysis consists of a comparison of an enterprise with current status with industry standards. It points our the firms's operating weaknesses, its potential, capacity, the volume and types of financing needed to enable the firm to accomplish the objectives of the management. Several types of financial ratios (the subject is discussed in detail under financial forecasting and planning under 'simple accounting procedure') may be applied as per requirement

1. Liquidity Ratio
2. Activities Ratio
3. Profitability Ratio
4. Leverage Ratio.

Re-payment: Proposed schedule of repayment of loads with required start-up period.
Receivables: An accounting term denoting the amounts owed the company.
Regulation: Governmental action sanctioned by law to control business behaviour.
Reserves: Monies held out of use by a company to meet certain demands or serve designated purposes, for example reserve for the replacement of worn out equipment.
Responsibility: Performance areas in which a person or unit is expected to produce results.
Result-producing-activities: Activities that produce measurable result that can be related, directly or indirectly, to the result and performance of the entire enterprise. Among result-producing activities are revenue-producing activities such as selling, non revenue activities such as manufacturing (result contributing activities), and information activities.
Return on investment (ROI): The ratio of the amount earned per year to the amount invested in a particular project or business (stated as a percentage).
Risk: The likelihood of success versus the likelihood of failure for any undertaking. Assessing a risk is the process of trying to quantify or judge which likelihood is the larger and by how much.

Security: In addition to the industrial assets of the unit, details relating to any other asset offered as security.
Scientific management: The approach of management fathered by Frederich W Taylor. Its core is the organised study of work, the analysis of into its simplest elements, and the systematic improvement of the work's performance of each of these elements, resulting in higher levels of output per worker.
Service institutions: Organisations constituted to perform a public task not involving the producing of a product. The service is provided in a nonprofit mode. Examples include the postal service, educational institutions and utility districts.
Service industries: Industries whose primary output is not provision of a manufactured product. Such industries are generally contrasted with manufacturing industries.
Simulation: An abstract replication of certain of the dynamics of a problem situation. The replication usually involves the manipulation of a model using a computer.
Simulated decentralization: A mode of organising large companies that are too big to

remain functionally organised and too integrated to be genuinely decentralised. One function or segment is treated as if it were an autonomous business relating to other units as if in an actual marketplace. The mode is typical in the materials, computer, chemical and pharmaceutical industries.

Social impacts: The societal consequences of actions that go beyond the consequences that are the action's *raison d'etre*.

Social psychology: The branch of psychology concerned with human behaviour in groups. The behaviour of the individual in the group and the behaviour of the group as a group are studied with the expectation that the results may be applied to improve individual and group performance.

Social responsibility: An institution's obligations to the society in which it resides. Recent discussion has highlighted differing points of view about what these obligations are.

Span of control: A number of persons who report directly to a given manager. In decades past, the question of whether this number had an upper limit or an ideal received much attention.

Speculation: Investments that have high likelihoods of failure but promise huge returns if successful.

Staff: individual contributors who advise or counsel rather than directly manage a group of people. Such persons are often contrasted with line managers.

Staffing: The management function that recruits, places, and trains the firm's resources.

Stock: Units of ownerships of a corporation.

Stockholders: The owners of the stock of a particular company. The stockholders are generally a very large group, but theoretically they exercise control over the company through a smaller board of directors.

Strategic planning: The planning for a company's long-term future that includes the setting of major overall objectives, the determination of the basic approaches to be used in pursuing these objectives, and the means to be used in obtaining the necessary resources to be employed.

Strategy: A company's basic approach to achieving its overall objectives.

Structure: The arrangement of processes and functions within the company as regards their relationships to each other. The methods used vary including the functional approach, decentralization, and matrix forms.

Suboptimization: Producing ideal performance in one area of a business and there by being unable to produce ideal or optimum performance for the business as whole.

Subordinate: A person who reports to a particular manager is said to be one of that manager's subordinate. Thus each line manager except the chief executive both has subordinates and is a subordinate.

Successor: The person who is appointed to a managerial position immediately after another person leaves the position is called the departing person's successor. The question of who the successors for top positions are to be frequently has great impact on a company's chances of success.

Supervisor: A person who has responsibility for directing the activities of a group of employees.

Support activities: Support activities include "conscience" activities (staff), and such functions as legal counsel, labour-relations activities. They are compared to result-activities, hygiene and housekeeping activities and top management activities.
Supporting capital: Working capital, that is, capital used to bring goods and services to market or to finance the time between their production and the time the buyer pays. Frequently contrasted with "producing" capital.
Surplus: Profits and other savings that successful performance can produce.
System: A set of interrelated parts. For example, one can speak about a distribution system, which might consist of a network of warehouses to be served in a particular manner by a number of plants and which, in turn, would ship to customers according to prescribed procedures.
System thinking: Analysis that uses systems and there dynamics to examine problems and possible solutions.

Tactics: Basic approaches to be used in carrying out a predetermined strategy.
Task force: A group assigned to accomplish a task. Committees may limit their attentions to making recommendations, while task forces are expected to perform a job.
Tax accounting: The subdivision of accounting that attends to keeping and summarizing records for tax purposes.
Team: A group of people who are expected to work together on a project.
Team organization: A mode of organization that creates and disbands teams for a succession of projects that constitute the majority of a firm's business.
Technology: A way or means to accomplish a task. The technology may or may not include the use of machines.
Technical feasibility: It encompasses the following elements:

1. Know-how: Source of know-how and payment of royalty/patent rights etc.
2. Process and quality control: A brief description of the process and arrangements of quality control.
3. Location: Location advantages with reference to raw materials, market, fuel, water, transport, labour, effluent disposal, permission from local bodies for setting up the industry.
4. Fixed assets: Land with area building, details of plant and machinery.
5. Raw materials: Major raw materials, source, quantity required per month and availability. If raw material is a restricted item, issue of permit/quota from concerned government agency.
6. Times Schedule: Expected completion period.

Technology assessment: The function of time to determine the impact of utilizing a particular technology in advance of its introduction. Proponents argue that technology assessment is possible. Opponents argue that it is impossible to technology in advance of its introduction.
Technology monitoring: Following the impacts of a technology as it is introduced in order to identify and combat the harmful impacts, if any. This process is recommended by some who think that technology assessment is difficult not impossible.

Theory X and Theory Y: Theories about human behaviour formulated by Douglas McGregor Theory X assumes that people are lazy, dislike and shun work, have to be driven, and need both carrot and stick. It assumes that most people are incapable of taking responsibility for themselves and have to be looked after. Theory Y assume that people have a psychological need to work and that they desire achievement and responsibility and will find them under the right conditions.

Term loans: Means a loan secured from any bank or financial Institution for acquiring fixed capital assets in the form of land, building, plan, machinery, tools implements and appliances etc.

Time and motion studies: Methods first promoted by the scientific management school. They include the study of physical work using stopwatches in order to break a task into segments that are redesigned in order to be performed more readily so that the productivity of the job is improved.

Time-sharing: A method of arranging the operating characteristics of a computer so that several users can be working on it at the same time. The term also refers to computing that a person does while the computer is set up in this way.

Top management: The managers who occupy the upper positions in the organizational hierarchy.

Total investment: 1. Cost of fixed assets proposed to be acquired and working capital requirements and other expenses.

2. Detail picture on bank loans, own investment and government margin money.

3. Credit on purchases.

Top-management activity: Activity that is to accomplish the top management tasks, which include thinking through the mission of the business, standard setting, building and maintenance of the human organization, major relation that only the people at the top of business can establish and maintain, "ceremonial" functions, and the provision of an organ to respond to major crises.

Trade associations: Organizations that bring the companies of an industry together for the purpose of exchanging information and jointly promoting the interests of the industry.

Union relations: The business of function conducting interactions with the unions to which a company's employees belong.

Union: An organization that brings workers in a trade or industry tighter for the purpose of bargaining collectively for improved wages, benefit, and working conditions.

Unity of Command: A management notion emphasized by early thinks. The concept states that each employee should have one and only one boss.

Utility: The usefulness or inherent value of something as perceived by an individual or an organization. A branch of economics tries to empirically measure and compare utilities.

Variable Costs: Costs of production process that vary with the level of production.

Wage and salary administration: The business function that determines wage and salary rates and adjusts them in response to market conditions and changed assignments.

Wealth: The sum total of economic valuables owned by an individual, a country, or a society.

Wholly-owned subsidiaries: Subsidiaries all of whose stock is owned by the parent company, as contrasted with a subsidiary that is controlled because of the parent's being the largest, but not the only, holder of stock in the subsidiary company.
Working capital: Supporting capital.
Yardsticks: Means of measuring results in key area of a business.
Zero-based budgeting: Budgeting that assumes that each project or activity must justify again any expenditures (above zero) for each new year even if the project or activity was justified previously.
Zero-sum games: Games in which the total of all winnings equals what is lost, that is, in which anything won resulted from a loss of one of the participants.

Source: People and performance by Peter F. Drucker

2. ABBREVIATIONS

CCIE : Chief Controller of Imports and Exports
CECD : Central Excise and Customs Department
CIF : Chief Inspector of Factories
CIPT : Central Institute of Plastic and Tools
CITD : Central Institute of Tool Design
CSIR : Council of Scientific and Industrial Research
DDCA : Directorate of Drug Control Administration
DEP : Directorate of Export Promotion
DGS&D : Director General of Supply and Disposal
DIC : District Industries Centre
DRDA : District Rural Development Agency
EB : Electricity Board
EDI : Entrepreneurship Development Institute of India
EDP : Entrepreneurship Development Program
EPC : Export Promotion Council
GMD : Geology and Mining Department
IC : Industries Commissioner
ICAR : Indian Council of Agriculture and Research
ICICI : Industrial Credit and Investment Corporation of India
ICMR : Indian Council of Medical Research
IDBI : Industrial Development Bank of India
IDC : Industrial Development Corporation
IFCI : Industrial Finance Corporation of India
IIC : Indian Investment Centre
IIFT : Indian Institute of Foreign Trade
IIM : Indian Institute of Management
IPB : Invention Promotion Board
IRL : Industrial Research Laboratory
ISI : Indian Standard Institute
LA : Local Authorities
LC : Leasing companies
MDC : Mineral Development Corporation
MID : Ministry of Industrial Development
MMTC : Mineral and Metals Trading Corporation
NABARD : National Bank for Agricultural Development
NIDC : Natural Institute of Development Corporation
NIESBUD : National Institute of Entrepreneurship and Small Business Development
NISIET : National Institute of Small Industry Extension Training
NRDC : National Research and Development Corporation
NSIC : National Small Industries Corporation
PTC : Polytechnology Transfer Centre
RC : Registration of Company

RIMCO	:	Rural Industries and Marketing Corporation
RTM	:	Registrar of Trade Marks
SBI	:	State Bank of India
SCB	:	Scheduled Commercial Banks
SEC	:	State Export Corporation
SFC	:	State Finance Corporation
SSIC	:	State Small Industries Corporation
SIDC	:	Small Industries Development Corporation
SISI	:	Small Industries Service Institute
SCPO	:	State Chemical and Pharmacuticals Organization
STC	:	State Trading Corporation
TC	:	Textile Commissioner
TCO	:	Technical Consultancy Organization
WPCB	:	Water Pollution Control Board
XISS	:	Xavier Institute of Social Service
XLRI	:	Xavier Labour Relations Institute

3. PROJECT REPORT PROFORMA*

Project Report on..

I. Introduction.

II. Name and address of the Entrepreneurs, Age Qualification, Experience & Family Back Ground.

III. Name of the proposed unit.

IV. Proposed site with details (Plot No. Mouza etc.) whether accommodation has been arranged or not.

V. (A) Products & Estimated production per annum (300 days) single shift basis.
(B) Process of manufacture.

VI. Requirement & availability of power & water.

VII. Communication facilities and other advantage to the site. Please enclose sketch plotting the road connection to the site indicating the main Bus Route & distance.

VIII. Availability & requirement of Raw material.

IX. Have you taken any loan from Govt./Financial Institution or other source? Please give details and loan still outstanding.

X. Marketability (Details of the area to be served, existing marketing channel, population, demand in the area, existing units with capacities, future prospects)

XI. Synopsis of the project cost:

(1) Fixed Capital		Rs. ______________
(2) Working Capital		Rs. ______________
	Total:	Rs. ______________

XII. Source of Finance:

	Fixed Capital	Working Capital	Total
1. WBFC/NSIC	Rs.	Rs.	Rs.
2. Bank	Rs.	Rs.	Rs.
3. Government	Rs.	Rs.	Rs.
4. Own	Rs.	Rs.	Rs.
Total –	Rs.	Rs.	Rs.

XIII. Cost Analysis

A. Fixed Capital

(*a*) (*i*) Land .... Area .... Leasehold/Rented/Rs. ....

(*ii*) Building .... Sft .... Rented .... Rs. ....

(*b*) Plant & Machines (with specification & Capacity)

	No.	Rate	Rs.
1.			
2.			
3.			
	Total		Rs.
Sales Tax & Surcharge			Rs.
	Total		Rs.

(*c*) Misc. tools, implements and auxiliaries Rs.

(*d*) Other expenses:

1. Furniture & Fixture
2. Security Deposit & Electrification
3. Transport Cost
4. Installation
5. Other preparative Expenses

Rs.

Fixed Capital (*a*), (*b*), (*c*) & (*d*) = Rs.
(Non-recurring Expenses)

B. Recurring Expenses (per month/season)

(*a*) Raw materials & Fuel Specification Quantity

Rate + Transport Cost Rs.

1.

2.

(*b*) Salary & Wages: Details of Staff No. Rate Rs.

(*c*) Other Recurring Expenses:

1. Rent
2. Electricity & Water
3. Consumable store, repair & maintenance
4. Packing & forwarding
5. T.A., Advt. & Office expenses
6. Misc Expenses

Total: Rs. ____________

Total Recurring

Expenses (per month) = a + b + c = Rs.

C. Working Capital requirement: Rs.

1. Raw material for 1 to 3 months
2. Salary & Wages for 1 to 3 months
3. Other Expenses for 1 to 3 months depending upon the type of industry/kind of activity

Total: Rs. ____________

D. Total investment: 1. Fixed Capital

2. Working Capital

Total: Rs. ____________

E. Profit & Loss Account (per month/season)

To	Rs.
1. Raw materials	By sale of
2. Salary & Wages	Details of products,
3. Other Rec. Exp.	quantity, rates, etc.
4. Dep. @10% 30% on M/C & Equip. per year	Rs.
5. Dep. on Building @5%	
6. Int. on loan @ 13% on Fixed Capital	
7. Int. @ 15% on Bank loan of Rs.	
8. Int. on Govt. Margin Money @ 4% per year	

9. Taxes and Insurance

Total: Rs. ____________

Profit: Rs. ____________ ____________

Total: Rs. ____________ Rs. ____________

F. Yearly appropriation of A/C	Yearly		
Repayment of Bank/WBFC/NSIC	Rs.	Profit	Rs.
Surplus before tax	Rs.	Add Dep.	Rs.
	Total: Rs.	Total:	Rs.

* Project Report Proforma Approved by the Govt. of W. Bengal.

4. SELF-RATING QUESTIONNAIRE FOR ENTREPRENEURS

The Self-Rating Questionnaire (SRO) consists of 70 brief statements. Using a five-point scale, respondents rate the degree to which each statement describes them. The scale is then scored to assess the strength of each of the 13 competencies. A total score across all the competencies provides an index of overall strength.

SRQ Administration

The Self-Rating Questionnaire can be self-administered or given orally. If it is self-administered, the instructions on the questionnaire explain how to complete it. If it is necessary to administer the questionnaire orally due to level of literacy, dialect or language differences, physical disabilities, or other practical problems, use the following guidelines:

1. Carefully read the instructions and ask questions to make sure the person understands how to complete the questionnaire.
2. Read each statement and then write down the number representing the person's choice next to the statement.
3. Read the five alternatives after each statement until you are certain that the respondent knows what each alternative is. You may need to continue this process for all 70 statements.

SRQ Scoring

After the questionnaire is completed, follow the instructions on the scoring sheet to calculate the scores for the 13 competencies and the total competency score. Then follow the Instructions on the SRQ Profile Sheet to make a graph of the competency scores that visually shows the relative competency strengths and weaknesses.

Self-Rating Questionnaire

Your Name ____

Company ____

Address ____

Date ____

Instructions

1. This questionnaire consists of 70 brief statements. Read each statement and decide how well it describes you. Be honest about yourself. Remember, no one does everything very well, nor is it even good to do everything very well, nor is it even good to do everything very well.
2. Select one of the numbers below to indicate how well the statement describes you:
   5 = Very well
   4 = Well
   3 = Somewhat
   2 = Very little
   1 = Not at all
3. Write the number you select on the line to the right of each statement. Here is an example:
   I remain calm in stressful situations. 2
   The person who responded to the item above wrote a "2" indicating that the statement described him very little.
4. Some statements may be similar but no two are exactly alike.
5. Please answer all questions.

Instructions: Select one of the numbers below to indicate how well each statement described you:

5 = Very well
4 = Well
3 = Somewhat
2 = Very little
1 = Not at all

Write the number on the line to the right of each statement.

1. I look for things that need to be done. ______
2. I like challenges and new opportunities. ______
3. When faced with a difficult problem, I spend a lot of time trying to find a solution. ______
4. When starting a new task or project, I gather a great deal of information. ______

5. It bothers me when things are not done very well. ______
6. I give much effort to my work. ______
7. I find ways to do things faster. ______
8. I plan a large project by breaking it down into smaller tasks. ______
9. I think of unusual solutions to problems. ______
10. I feel confident that I will succeed at whatever I try to do. ______
11. I tell others when they have not performed as expected. ______
12. I get others to support my recommendations. ______
13. I develop strategies to influence others. ______
14. No matter who I'm talking to, I'm a good listener.
15. I do things that need to be done before being asked to by others. ______
16. I prefer activities that I know well and with which I am comfortable. ______
17. I try several times to get people to do what I would like them to do. ______

Instructions: Select one of the numbers below to indicate how well each statement describes you:

5 = Very well
4 = Well
3 = Somewhat
2 = Very little
1 = Not at all

Write the number on the line to the right of each statement.

18. I seek the advice of people who know a lot about the problems or tasks I am working on. ______
19. It is important to me to do a high quality job. ______
20. I work long hours and make personal sacrifices to complete jobs on time. ______
21. I am not good at using my time well.
22. I think about the advantages and disadvantages of different ways of accomplishing things. ______
23. I think of many new ideas. ______
24. I change my mind if others disagree strongly with me. ______
25. If I am angry or upset with someone, I tell that person. ______
26. I convince others of my ideas. ______
27. I do not spend much time thinking about how to influence others. ______
28. I feel resentful when I don't get my way. ______
29. I do things before it is clear that they must be done. ______

30. I notice opportunities to do new things. ______
31. When something gets in the way of what I am trying to do, I keep on trying to accomplish what I want. ______
32. I take action without seeking information. ______
33. My own work is better than that of other people I work with. ______
34. I do whatever it takes to complete a job. ______
35. It bothers me when may time is wasted. ______

Instructions: Select one of the numbers below to indicate how well each statement describes you:

5 = Very well
4 = Well
3 = Somewhat
2 = Very little
1 = Not at all

Write the number on the line to the right of each statement.

36. I try to think of all the problems I may encounter and plan what to do if each problem occurs. ______
37. Once I have selected an approach to solving a problem, I do not change that approach. ______
38. When trying something difficult or challenging, I feel confident that I will succeed. ______
39. It is difficult for me to order people to do things. ______
40. I get others to see how I will be able to accomplish what I set out to do. ______
41. I get important people to help me accomplish my goals. ______
42. In the past, I have had failures. ______
43. I take action before it is clear that I must. ______
44. I try things that are very new and different from what I have done before. ______
45. When faced with a major difficulty, I quickly go on to other things. ______
46. When working on a project for someone, I ask many questions to be sure I understand what that person wants. ______
47. When something I have been working on is satisfactory, I do not spend extra time trying to make it better. ______
48. When I am doing a job for someone, I make a special effort to make sure that person is satisfied with my work. ______
49. I find ways to do things for less cost. ______

50. I deal with problems as they arise, rather than spend time trying to anticipate them. ______

51. I think of many ways to solve problems. ______

Instructions: Select one of the numbers below to indicate how well each statement describes you:

5 = Very well
4 = Well
3 = Somewhat
2 = Very little
1 = Not at all

Write the number on the line to the right of each statement.

52. I do things that are risky. ______

53. When I disagree with others, I let them know. ______

54. I am very persuasive with others. ______

55. In order to reach my goals, I think of solutions that benefit everyone involved in a problem. ______

56. There have been occasions when I took advantage of someone. ______

57. I wait for direction from others before taking action. ______

58. I take advantage of opportunities that arise. ______

59. I try several ways to overcome things that get in the way of reaching my goals. ______

60. I go to several different sources to get information to help with tasks or projects. ______

61. I want the company I own to be the best of its type. ______

62. I do not let my work interfere with my family or personal life. ______

63. I get the most I can out of the money I have to accomplish a project or task. ______

64. I take a logical and systematic approach to activities. ______

65. If one approach to a problem does not work, I think of another approach. ______

66. I stick with my decisions even if others disagree strongly with me. ______

67. I tell people what they have to do, even if they do not want to do it. ______

68. I cannot get people who have strong opinions or ideas to change their minds. ______

Instructions: Select one of the numbers below to indicate how well each statement describes you:

5 = Very well
4 = Well
3 = Somewhat
2 = Very little
1 = Not at all

Write the number on the line to the right of each statement.

69. I get to know people who may be able to help me reach my goals. _____
70. When I don't know something, I don't mind admitting it. _____

SCORING SHEET FOR SELF-RATING QUESTIONNAIRE

Instructions: 1. Enter the ratings from the completed questionnaire on the lines above the item numbers in parentheses. Notice that the item numbers in each column are consecutive: item number 2 is below item number 1, and so forth.

2. Do the addition and subtraction indicated in each row to compute each competency score.

3. Add all competency scores to compute the total score.

Ratings of Statements	Score	Competency
___ (1) + ___ (15) + ___ (29) + ___ (43) − ___ (57) + 6	= _____	Initiative
___ (2) − ___ (16) + ___ (30) + ___ (44) + ___ (58) + 6	= _____	Sees & Acts on Opportunities
___ (3) + ___ (17) + ___ (31) − ___ (45) + ___ (59) + 6	= _____	Persistence
___ (4) + ___ (18) − ___ (32) + ___ (46) + ___ (60) + 6	= _____	Information Seeking
___ (5) + ___ (19) + ___ (33) − ___ (47) + ___ (61) + 6	= _____	Concern for High Quality of Work
___ (6) + ___ (20) + ___ (34) + ___ (48) − ___ (62) + 6	= _____	Commitment to Work Contract
___ (7) − ___ (21) + ___ (35) + ___ (49) − ___ (63) + 6	= _____	Efficiency Orientation
___ (8) + ___ (22) + ___ (36) − ___ (50) + ___ (64) + 6	= _____	Systematic Planning

(9) + (23) − (37) + (51) + (65) + 6 = ______ Problem Solving

(10) − (24) + (38) + (52) + (66) + 6 = ______ Self-Confidence

(11) + (25) − (39) + (53) + (67) + 6 = ______ Assertiveness

(12) + (26) + (40) + (54) − (68) + 6 = ______ Persuasion

(13) − (27) + (41) + (55) − (69) + 6 = ______ Use of Influence Strategies

Total score = ______

(14) − (28) − (42) − (56) + (70) + 18 = ______ Correction Factor

CORRECTED SCORING SHEET

Instructions

1. The Correction Factor (the total of items 14, 28, 42, 56 and 70) is used to determine whether or not a person tries to present a very favorable image of himself. If the total score on this factor is 20 or greater, then the total scores on the 13 competencies must be corrected to provide a more accurate assessment of the strength of the competencies for that individual.
2. Use the following numbers when figuring the corrected score:

If the Correction Factor score is:	Subtract the following number from the total score for each competency:
24 or 25	7
22 or 23	5
20 or 21	3
19 or less	0

3. Use the next page to correct each competency before using the Profile Sheet.

CORRECTED SCORE SHEET

Competency	Original Score	Correction Number	=	Corrected Total
Initiative	_____	–	=	_____
Sees and Acts on Opportunities	_____	–	=	_____
Persistence	_____	–	=	_____
Information Seeking	_____	–	=	_____
Concern for High Quality of Work	_____	–	=	_____
Commitment to Work Contract	_____	–	=	_____
Efficiency Orientation	_____	–	=	_____
Systematic Planning	_____	–	=	_____
Problem Solving	_____	–	=	_____
Self-Confidence	_____	–	=	_____
Assertiveness	_____	–	=	_____
Persuasion	_____	–	=	_____
Use of Influence strategies	_____	–	=	_____
		Corrected Total Score		_____

COMPETENCY PROFILE SHEET FOR SELF-RATING QUESTIONNAIRE

Instructions

1. Transfer the corrected competency score to the profile sheet by marking an "X" at the appropriate point on the dotted horizontal line for each competency.
2. Draw a heavy line over the dotted horizontal line for each competency, from the left vertical line to the point you have marked with an "X". The heavy lines you have drawn graphically represent the strength of each competency.
3. The following is an example of how to create the profile sheet.
   If the score for Initiative is 19, it will appear as follows:

Initiative

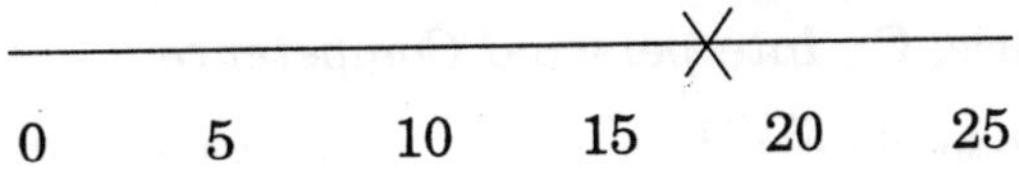

PROFILE SHEET

Competency

Initiative

Sees and Acts on Opportunities

Persistence

Information Seeking

Concern for High Quality of Work

Commitment to Work Contract

Efficiency Orientation

Systematic Planning

Problem Solving

Self-Confidence

Assertiveness

Persuasion

Use of Influence strategies

References

1. Argyaris, C., *Interpersonal Competence*
2. F.R. Bogaert MVD, SJ & S.P. Das, *Group Entrepreneurship with Rural Poor*
3. Donglass Mc Gregor, *Live management Responsibility for Human Relations*
4. Drucker, P., *Practice of Management*
5. Engel J.F. David, T. Kollat and Roger, D. Blackwell, *Consumer Behavior*
6. Herzberg F., B. Mausuer and Barbara Snyderman, *The Motivation to Work*
7. Joel Dean, *Managerial Economics*
8. Kotler Philip, *Marketing Management, Analysis, Planning and Control*
9. Katz & R.L. Kahn, *The Social Psychology of Organisation*
10. Koontz, H. & C. O'Donnel, *Principles of Management*
11. Likert, R., *The human organisation: It's Management and Value*
12. Lippit, R. Jeannew Watson & Bruce Westley, *The Dynamics of Planned Change*
13. Levin Rechard, I. & C. O. Kirkpatric, *Quantitative Approaches to Management*
14. Massie J.L., *Essentials of Management*
15. Mc Lelland, D.C., *The Achieving Society*
16. Maslow, A.H., *The Theory of Human Motivation*
17. Mc Gregor, D., *The Human side of Enterprise*
18. Sherlekar, S.A., *Marketing Management*
19. Stanton, W., *Fundamentals of Marketing*
20. Schumpeter, J.A., *Capitalism, Socialism and Democracy*
21. Sayles & Leonard, *Managerial Behaviour*
22. Taylor, F. W., *Scientific Management*
23. Urwick, L., *Notes on Theory of Organization*
24. USA Small Business Administration, *The State of Small Business*
25. William H. Newman, Charles E. Summer and E. Kirby Warren, *The Process of Management: Concepts, Behavior and Practice.*